Critters
of New York

Pocket Guide to Animals in Your State

ALEX TROUTMAN

produced in cooperation with
Wildlife Forever

About Wildlife Forever

Wildlife Forever works to conserve America's outdoor heritage through conservation education, preservation of habitat, and scientific management of fish and wildlife. Wildlife Forever is a 501c3 nonprofit organization dedicated to restoring habitat and teaching the next generation about conservation. Become a member and learn more about innovative programs like the Art of Conservation®, The Fish and Songbird Art Contests®, Clean Drain Dry Initiative™, and Prairie City USA®. For more information, visit wildlifeforever.org.

Thank you to Ann McCarthy, the original creator of the Critters series, for her dedication to wildlife conservation and to environmental education. Ann dedicates her work to her daughters, Megan and Katharine Anderson.

Front cover photos by **Josh14/shutterstock.com:** American woodcock, **Jay Ondreicka/shutterstock.com:** bog turtle, **Gaston Piccinetti/shutterstock.com:** bobcat
Back cover photo by **Ian Peter Morton/Shutterstock.com:** northern river otter

Edited by Brett Ortler and Jenna Barron
Cover and book design by Jonathan Norberg
Proofreader: Emily Beaumont

10 9 8 7 6 5 4 3 2 1

Critters of New York
First Edition 2005, Second Edition 2024

Published by Adventure Publications
An imprint of AdventureKEEN
310 Garfield Street South, Cambridge, Minnesota 55008
(800) 678-7006
www.adventurepublications.net
All rights reserved
Printed in China
Cataloging-in-Publication data is available from the Library of Congress
ISBN 978-1-64755-433-0 (pbk.); 978-1-64755-434-7 (ebook)

Acknowledgments

I want to thank everyone who believed in and supported me over the years—a host of friends, family, and teachers. I want to especially thank my mom and my siblings Van, Bre, and TJ.

Dedication

I dedicate this book to my brother Van:
May you continue to enjoy the birds and wildlife in heaven.

This book is for all the kids who have a passion for nature and the outdoors, especially ones who identify as Black, Brown, Indigenous, and People of Color. May this be an encouragement to never give up. And if you have a dream and passion for something, pursue it relentlessly. I also hope to set an example that you can be successful as your full, authentic self!

Lastly, I dedicate this book to all those with ADHD and dyslexia, as well as all other members of the neurodivergent community. While our quirks make things more challenging, our goals are not impossible to reach; sometimes it takes a little more time and help, but we, too, can succeed!

Contents

Reptiles and Amphibians

Introduction

My passion for nature started when I was young. I was always amazed by the sunlit fiery glow of the red-tailed hawks as they soared overhead when I went fishing with my family. The red-tailed hawk was my spark bird—the bird that captures your attention and gets you into birding. Through my many encounters with red-tailed hawks, and other species like garter snakes and coyotes, I found a passion for nature and the environment. Stumbling across conservationists like Steve Irwin, Jeff Corwin, and Jack Hanna introduced me to the field of Wildlife Biology as a career and gave birth to a dream that I was able to accomplish and live out: serving as a Fish and Wildlife Biologist for governmental agencies, as well as in the private sector.

My childhood dream was driven by a desire to learn more about the different types of ecosystems and the animals that call our wild places home. Books and field guides like this one whet my thirst for knowledge. Even before I could fully understand the words on the pages, I was drawn to books and flashcards that had animals on them. I could soon identify every animal I was shown and tell a fact about it. I hope that this edition of *Critters of New York* can be the fuel that sustains your passion for not only learning about wildlife but also for caring for the environment and making sure that all are welcome in the outdoors. For others, may this book be the spark that ignites a flame for wildlife preservation and environmental stewardship. I hope that this book inspires children from lower socioeconomic and minority backgrounds to pursue their dreams to the fullest and be unapologetically themselves.

By profession, I'm a Fish and Wildlife Biologist, and I'm a nature enthusiast through and through. My love for nature includes making sure that everyone has an equal opportunity to enjoy the outdoors in their own way. So, as you use this book, I encourage you to be intentional in inviting others to appreciate nature with you. Enjoy your discoveries and stay curious!

–Alex Troutman

New York: The Empire State

When you think of New York, the Big Apple–New York City–probably comes to mind. But the state is known for so much more than just the Statue of Liberty and Times Square. More than 10,000 years ago, Indigenous people came to what is now called New York, later becoming the tribes such as the Cayuga, Mohawk, Oneida, and Seneca. Many years later, the Dutch colony of New Amsterdam was created in the area; it was later taken over by the British. New York formally became part of the United States in 1788, when it was the 11th state to join the Union.

New York touches Canada and Lake Ontario to the north. The northeastern part of the state has the Adirondack Mountains, which are protected as a state park. There are several animals that call the Adirondacks their home, including black bears, martins, woodpeckers, common loons, and eastern newts. In the south, the state touches the Atlantic Ocean, where animals like humpback whales and harbor seals thrive.

These environments are home to many animals, including around 90 species of mammals, 450-some species of birds, and more than 70 species of reptiles and amphibians, not to mention fish, countless insects and spiders, mushrooms, plants, and more. This is your guide to the animals, birds, reptiles, and amphibians that call New York home.

Some of New York's most iconic plants, animals, and other natural resources are now officially recognized as state symbols. Get to know them below and see if you can spot them all! You'll probably encounter the state nickname and motto, so I've included them here too.

State Bird: eastern bluebird

State Mammal: beaver

 State Tree: sugar maple

State Flower: wild rose

State Fish: brook trout

State Insect: ladybug

 State Reptile: common snapping turtle

State Shell: bay scallop

State Nickname: The Empire State

State Motto: "Excelsior, E Pluribus Unum" (Ever Upward, Out of Many One)

How to Use This Guide

This book is your introduction to some of the wonderful critters found in New York; it includes 21 mammals, 32 birds, and 12 reptiles and amphibians. It includes some animals you probably already know, such as deer and bald eagles, but others you may not know about, such as queen snakes or bobolinks. I've selected the species in this book because they are wide-spread (northern raccoon, page 42), abundant (black-capped chickadee, page 68), or well-known but best observed from a safe distance (common snapping turtle, page 134).

The book is organized by types of animals: mammals, birds, and reptiles and amphibians. Within each section, the animals are in alphabetical order. If you'd like to look for a critter quickly, turn to the checklist (page 140), which you can also use to keep track of how many animals you've seen! For each species, you'll see a photo of the animal, along with neat facts and information on the animal's habitat, diet, its predators, how it raises its young, and more.

Safety Note

Nature can be unpredictable, so don't go outdoors alone, and always tell an adult when you're going outside. All wild animals should be treated with respect. If you see one—big or small—don't get close to it or attempt to touch or feed it. Instead, keep your distance and enjoy spotting it. If you can, snap some pictures with a camera or make a quick drawing using a sketchbook. If the animal is getting too close, is acting strangely, or seems sick or injured, tell an adult right away, as it might have rabies, a disease that can affect mammals. The good news is there's a rabies vaccine, so it's important to visit a doctor right away if you get bit or scratched by a wild animal.

Notes About Icons

Each species page includes basic information about an animal, from what it eats to how it survives the winter. The book also includes information that's neat to know; in the mammals section, each page includes a simple track illustration of the animal, with approximate track size included. And along the bottom, there is an example track pattern for the mammal, with the exception for those that primarily glide or fly (flying squirrels and bats).

On the left-hand page for each mammal, a rough-size illustration is included that shows how big the animal is when compared to a basketball.

Also on the left-hand page, there are icons that tell you when each animal is most active: nocturnal (at night), diurnal (during the day), or crepuscular (at dawn/dusk), so you know when to look. If an animal has a "zzz" icon, it hibernates during the winter. Some animals hibernate every winter, and their internal processes (breathing and heartbeat) slow down almost entirely. Other animals only partially hibernate, but this still helps them save energy and survive through the coldest part of the year.

nocturnal
(active at night)

diurnal
(active during day)

crepuscular
(most active at dawn and dusk)

hibernates/deep sleeper
(dormant during winter)

ground nest   cup nest   platform nest   cavity nest   migrates

On the left-hand side of each bird page, the nest for the species is shown, along with information on whether or not the bird migrates; on the right-hand side, there's information on where it goes.

Did you know?

Beavers are rodents! Yes, these flat-tailed mammals are rodents, like rats and squirrels. In fact, they are the largest native rodents in North America. Just like other rodents, beavers have large incisors, which they use to chew through trees to build dams and dens. Beavers are the original wetland engineers. By damming rivers and streams, beavers create ponds and wetlands.

Size Comparison   Most Active   Track Size

6"

American Beaver

Castor canadensis

Size: Body is 25–30 inches long; tail is 9–13 inches long; weighs 30–70 pounds

Habitat: Wooded wetland areas near ponds, streams, and lakes

Range: Beavers can be found throughout New York and in much of the rest of the United States.

Food: Leaves, twigs, and stems; they also feed on fruits and aquatic plant roots. Throughout the year they gather and store tree cuttings, which they eat in winter.

Den: A beaver's home is called a lodge. It consists of a pile of branches that is splattered with mud and vegetation. Lodges are constructed on the banks of lakes and streams and have exits and entrances that are underwater.

Young: Young beavers (kits) are born in late April through May and June in litters of 3–4. After two years they are considered mature and will be forced out of the den.

Predators: Bobcats, cougars, bears, wolves, and coyotes. Human trappers are major predators too.

Tracks: A beaver's front foot looks a lot like your hand; it has five fingers. The hind (back) foot is long, with five separate toes that have webbing or extra skin between them.

Beavers range from dark brown to reddish brown. They have a stocky body with hind legs that are longer than the front legs. The beaver's body is covered in dense fur, but its tail is naked and has special blood vessels that help it cool or warm its body.

Did you know?

A group of martens is called a richness. Martens will dig tunnels under the snow in winter in order to stay warm. While they are in the weasel family, they are not as long as weasels.

Size Comparison   Most Active   Track Size 1⅛–2¼"

American Marten

Martes americana

Size: 20–26 inches long; weighs 1½–3 pounds

Habitat: Woodlands and forests

Range: In New York, they are limited to the area around Adirondack Park. They can also be found in Alaska and Canada, south to northern New Mexico, and in parts of California.

Food: Omnivores that feed on red squirrels, fruits, birds, seeds, fish, frogs, berries, beech nuts, insects, and carrion (dead animals)

Den: Give birth in dens lined with grass, moss, and leaves. After birth, they move young (kits) to a maternal den.

Young: Kits are born in March and April and are fully grown within 3 months. A few weeks to months later, the mother will leave. They reach reproductive maturity at 2 years.

Predators: Fishers, great horned owls, golden eagles, coyotes, and red foxes. Humans in the form of trapping

Tracks: Front track is 1¼–2½ inches long and wide; hind track is 1⅛–2¼ inches. They have five toes on each foot with sharp claws that are semi-retractable.

Martens are slender mammals that have a long, fluffy tail; big ears; and a small, pointed face. They have long, soft fur in variations of buff browns and reds; a pale face and chest; and dark feet and tail tip. The tail is ⅓ of its overall size.

Did you know?

Female bears weigh between 90 and 300 pounds and are smaller than the average adult human male in the US. But don't let their small size fool you; with a bite force around 800 pounds per square inch (PSI) and a swiping force of over 400 pounds, these bears are not to be taken lightly.

Size Comparison   Most Active   Track Size   Hibernates

6–7"

Black Bear
Ursus americanus

Size: 5–6 feet long (nose to tail); weighs 90–600 pounds

Habitat: Forests, mountains, lowland areas, and swamps

Range: In New York, they can be found throughout the state in areas away from the "big city." They are found in much of North America, from northern Canada down into Mexico.

Food: Berries, fish, crops, small mammals, wild grapes, tree shoots, ants, bees, and even deer fawns

Den: Denning usually starts in December, with bears emerging in late March or April. Dens can be either dug (out of a hillside, for example) or constructed with materials such as leaves, grass, and moss.

Young: Two cubs are usually born at one time (a litter), often in January. Cubs are born blind and without fur, with pink skin. They weigh 8–16 ounces.

Predators: Humans and other bears. Sometimes, other carnivores, such as mountain lions, wolves, coyotes, or even bobcats, will prey on black bears. Cubs are especially vulnerable.

Tracks: Front print is usually 4–6 inches long and 3½–5 inches wide, with the hind foot being 6–7 inches long and 3½–5 inches wide. The feet have five toes.

Black bears are usually black in color, but they can be many different variations of black and brown. Some even have grayish, reddish, or blond fur.

Did you know?

Bobcats get their name from their short tail; a "bob" is a type of short haircut. They have the largest range of all wild cats in the United States. Bobcats can even hunt prey much larger than themselves; in fact, they can take down prey that is over four times their size, such as white-tailed deer!

Size Comparison   Most Active   Track Size

Bobcat

Lynx rufus

Size: 27–48 inches head to tail; males weigh around 30 pounds, while females weigh 24 pounds or so.

Habitat: Dense forests, scrub areas (forests of low trees and bushes), swamps, and even some urban (city) areas

Range: In New York, they have been found throughout the state; they are widespread throughout the United States.

Food: Squirrels, birds, rabbits and snowshoe hares, and white-tailed deer fawns; occasionally even adult deer and porcupines!

Den: Dense shrubs, caves, or even hollow trees; dens can be lined with leaves or moss.

Young: Bobcats usually breed in early winter through spring. Females give birth to a litter of 2–4 kittens. Bobcats become independent around 7–8 months, and they reach reproductive maturity at 1 year for females and at 2 years for males.

Predators: Occasionally fishers and coyotes; humans also hunt and trap bobcats for fur.

Tracks: Roughly 2 inches wide; both front and back paws have four toe pads and a carpal pad (a pad below the toe pads).

Bobcats have a white belly and a brown or pale-gray top with black spots. The tail usually has a black tip. They are mostly crepuscular (say it, cre-pus-cue-lar), which means they are most active in the dawn and twilight hours.

Did you know?
At one time, coyotes were only found in the central and western parts of the US, but now, with the help of humans (eliminating predators and clearing forests), they can be found throughout most of the country.

Size Comparison   Most Active   Track Size

2"

Coyote
Canis latrans

Size: 3–4 feet long; weighs 21–50 pounds

Habitat: Urban and suburban areas, woodlands, grasslands, and farm fields

Range: Coyotes can be found in all the counties of New York. Even though they are mostly found in rural areas, they can also be seen in larger city areas. They are found throughout the US and Mexico, the northern parts of Central America, and southern Canada.

Food: A variety of prey, including rodents, birds, deer, and sometimes livestock

Den: Coyotes will dig their own dens but will often use old fox or badger dens or hollow logs.

Young: 5–7 pups, independent around 8–10 months

Predators: Bears and wolves; humans trap and kill for pelts and to "protect" livestock.

Tracks: Four toes and a carpal pad (the single pad below the toe pads) can be seen on all four feet.

Coyotes have brown, reddish-brown, or gray back fur with a lighter gray-to-white belly. They have a longer muzzle than other wild canines. They are active mostly during the night (nocturnal) but also during the twilight and dawn hours (crepuscular).

Did you know?

Chipmunks get their English name from the "chip" or alert calls they use when they sense a threat. Eastern chipmunks are not fully herbivores (plant eaters); in fact, they eat a variety of things, including other mammals and amphibians, like frogs.

Size Comparison   Most Active   Track Size   Hibernates

Eastern Chipmunk

Tamias striatus

Size: Body is 3–6 inches long; tail is 3–4 inches long; weighs 2½–5½ ounces

Habitat: Suburban areas, woodlands, and dense scrub areas

Range: Found throughout New York, the eastern US, and southern Canada

Food: Berries, nuts, seeds, frogs, insects

Den: Has multiple chambers (or rooms); the entrance is usually hidden under brush, fallen trees, rock piles, and human-made landscaping items.

Young: 2–8 young (kits) per litter, 2 litters per year. Born blind and without fur. Weigh under an ounce at birth. Eyes open at 4 weeks, becomes independent at 8 weeks

Predators: Coyotes, feral and outdoor house cats, snakes, weasels, bobcats, hawks, and owls

Tracks: The front foot has four digit (toe) pads and is ½ inch long; the hind foot has five digit pads and is just under ¾ inch.

Chipmunks are small rodents with brown base colors, seven alternating stripes, and white bellies. During winter, they will stay underground. They hide food in underground caches that they will feed on through the winter.

Did you know?

The eastern cottontail gets its name from its short, puffy tail that looks like a cotton ball. A cottontail can travel up to 18 miles per hour! Rabbits have great hearing and eyesight. They can almost see all the way around them (360 degrees). On days with high wind, they will bed down in a burrow because the wind interferes with their ability to hear and detect predators.

Size Comparison   Most Active   Track Size

3½"

24

Eastern Cottontail

Sylvilagus floridanus

Size: 16–19 inches long; weighs 1½–4 pounds

Habitat: Forests, swamps, orchards, deserts, and farm areas

Range: Found throughout New York except the areas of the Adirondacks that lack adequate brush habitat for them; through the eastern US to Arizona and New Mexico; isolated ranges in the Pacific Northwest

Food: Clovers; grasses; wild strawberries; garden plants; and twigs of a variety of trees, including maple, oak, and sumac

Den: Rabbits don't dig dens; they bed in shallow, grassy, saucer-shaped depressions (holes) or under shrubs. They will sometimes use woodchuck dens in the winter.

Young: They usually have 2–4 kits at one time, but it's not uncommon to have 7 or more. Born naked and blind, they weigh about an ounce (about the same weight as a slice of bread) and gain weight very quickly.

Predators: Owls, coyotes, eagles, weasels, humans, and foxes

Tracks: The front foot is an inch long with four toe pads; the hind foot is 3½ inches long.

An eastern cottontail sports thick brown fur with a white belly, a gray rump, and a white "cotton" tail. During the winter, it survives by eating bark off of fruit trees and shrubs.

Did you know?

The eastern fox squirrel's bones appear pink under ultraviolet (UV) light, a type of light human eyes can't see. Squirrels accidentally help plant trees by forgetting where they have previously buried nuts. Sometimes, they seem to pretend to bury nuts to throw off would-be nut thieves.

Size Comparison   Most Active   Track Size
2½"

Eastern Fox Squirrel

Sciurus niger

Size: 19–28 inches long; weighs 1–3 pounds

Habitat: Open woodlands, suburban areas, and dense forests

Range: They are found throughout the western part of New York State and the eastern United States to Texas and as far north as the Dakotas.

Food: Acorns, seeds, nuts, insects such as moths and beetles, birds, eggs, and dead fish

Den: Ball-shaped dreys, or nests, are made of vegetation like leaves, sometimes in tree cavities.

Young: 2–3 kits are born between late January to April and late June through August. Kittens are born naked and weigh half an ounce; they are cared for by their parents for the first 7–8 weeks. They can reproduce by around 10–11 months for males and 8 months for females.

Predators: Humans, hawks, cats, coyotes, bobcats, and weasels

Tracks: The front tracks have four digits (toes), and the hind feet have five digits.

The eastern fox squirrel is the largest tree squirrel in New York. It is gray or reddish brown with a yellowish or light-brown underside. There is also a rare black and smoky-gray color phase. Both the male and female look the same.

Did you know?

Harbor seals are one of the most common marine mammals to be seen on the coast! Due to their pelvic bones being fused, they are unable to move their hind (back) flippers to walk; instead, they use caterpillar-like movements to cross land.

Size Comparison   Most Active

Harbor Seal

Phoca vitulina

Size: 5–6 feet long; weighs 90–350 pounds (or more for males)

Habitat: Coastal areas such as sandy beaches; tidal mudflats; sand bars; and exposed, rocky shorelines

Range: They are found along the New York coast and the entire eastern coast to Florida and down the western coast of the United States.

Food: Fish, shellfish, and crustaceans

Den: Aquatic mammals do not den.

Young: Pups weighing about 24 pounds are born around 10 months after breeding and can swim minutes after being born. They drink their mother's milk for up to 6 weeks and reach reproductive maturity at 3–7 years.

Predators: Killer whales; great white and Greenland sharks and possibly other shark species; Steller sea lions; walrus; eagles; gulls; and ravens

Tracks: They have webbed front feet with five toes, or digits, on them. Hind tracks are rarely left due to limited movement on land.

Harbor seals are brown, gray, or variations of browns and grays; some even have splotches or rings on them. They have stout, round bodies with short flippers. They have big heads with nostrils that are chevron- or V-shaped. They do not have external ear flaps like similar species, such as sea lions.

Did you know?

The humpback whale gets its name from the large hump on its back. Humpback whales come in various color patterns, and the spots and scars on their tail fluke can help researchers identify individuals. Its front fins can be over 15 feet long, up to a third of its total length.

Size Comparison   Most Active

Humpback Whale

Megaptera novaeangliae

Size: 48–63 feet long; weighs 80,000 pounds, or 40 tons

Habitat: Open water; visitors to bays and harbors

Range: Can be found in every ocean. In New York, can be seen along the coast as well as in the open ocean

Food: They are carnivores that mainly eat krill and fish.

Den: No den; gives live birth in the ocean

Young: After 11½ months of pregnancy, females usually give birth to one calf that is over 10 feet long and weighs over 1,000 pounds. After 5–7 months, calves are weaned and will remain with their mom for a year. Humpback whales are reproductively mature around 4–5 years old.

Predators: Humans (boat strikes), killer whales, and large sharks

Tracks: Fully aquatic animals with flippers; no tracks are left.

Humpback whales sport a black upper body and white underside. They have over 20 grooves running down their throat and underside. Humpback whales are stout and have long flippers and a short dorsal fin. Flippers and fluke (tail) are jagged.

Did you know?
The Indiana bat gets its name because the first known specimen was observed in a cave in southern Indiana in 1904. One New York mine is the roosting location for half of the Indiana bats of the northeast. They can roost in large groups as dense as 300 bats per square foot.

Size Comparison   Most Active   Hibernates

Indiana Bat

Myotis sodalis

Size: 2 inches long; wingspan of 10 inches; weighs ¼ ounce

Habitat: Grasslands, caves, mines, woodlands, and wetlands

Range: They can be found as far north as Vermont, west to Arkansas, and as far south as Florida. In New York, they can be found in the central and eastern areas of the state.

Food: Insectivore; eats flies, moths, caddisflies, and beetles

Den: Females roost in colonies of up to 100 individuals. Roosts are in crevices of trees or under bark.

Young: Females have one pup a year, and the pup learns to fly within a month.

Predators: Snakes, raccoons, and owls

Tracks: Although they are rarely on the ground to leave a track, it would show one thumbprint on the forearms and the hind footprint.

The Indiana bat is a small, fluffy, grayish-brown bat. Its nose is usually pink. Indiana bats use different roosting techniques during the summer and winter; during the summer, they roost in trees in the forest, and during the winter, they hibernate in caves or mines.

The Indiana bat does not often leave tracks.

Did you know?

Weasels are small but tough! They will attack prey over three times their own size, and they help control rodent and pest species by eating mice, voles, and other small mammals.

Size Comparison   Most Active   Track Size

Long-tailed Weasel

Mustela frenata

Size: 14–18 inches long; weighs 5 ounces to 1 pound

Habitat: Forests, farms, and rocky areas

Range: Weasels can be found throughout New York and the rest of the United States, except for a small pocket in southern California, Nevada, and Arizona.

Food: Ducks and other birds, frogs, rodents, rabbits, and sometimes domesticated chickens and eggs; they will hide extra food to eat later.

Den: Weasels will dig dens but will also use rock piles, abandoned burrows of other animals, or hollow logs. Dens are covered with fur and grass.

Young: 4–8 kits are born in April; they reach adult weight within 4 months.

Predators: Hawks, owls, coyotes, foxes, humans, and cats

Tracks: The front foot is wider than the hind foot. Each foot has five toe pads with four claws extending from them.

Long-tailed weasels have several color phases, including alternating from brown to white as the seasons change from summer to winter.

Did you know?

Mink have webbed feet, like otters. Although they usually dive and swim short distances, mink can dive over 13 feet deep and swim for over 95 feet underwater, if necessary!

Size Comparison   Most Active   Track Size

1¾"

Mink
Mustela vison

Size: 16–27 inches long; weighs 1½–3½ pounds

Habitat: Wetland areas with dense vegetation near streams, lakes, and swamps

Range: They are found across much of New York (though are mainly seen in less-populated areas), as well as throughout most of the US and Canada.

Food: Fish, eggs, snakes, muskrats, farm animals, small mammals, and aquatic animals such as crayfish

Den: Their dens are near water, in holes in the ground, hollow logs, and old muskrat and beaver lodges; they will use grass or fur from prey as bedding.

Young: At birth, they weigh less than an ounce; mothers give birth to 3–6 young, called kits. They are mature at 1 year old.

Predators: Otters, birds of prey, wolves, coyotes, bobcats, internal parasites, and humans (who trap them for fur)

Tracks: Both the front and hind tracks resemble a gloved hand. Both the left and right tracks are seen parallel to each other because the mink often bound (leap) when moving. Tracks are usually seen near water.

A mostly nocturnal (active at night) animal, it has a shiny or glossy dark-brown coat that it keeps all year long. Mink usually have a white or pale-yellow chest patch or bib on the throat that sometimes extends to the belly.

Did you know?

Moose belong to the deer family, and they are the largest members of the deer family in the world! They can rotate their ears 180 degrees. Moose can swim over 5 miles per hour for over 8 miles, and they can also run over 35 miles per hour. Moose will dive beneath the water of ponds and lakes to reach the plants at the bottom.

Size Comparison

Most Active

Track Size

5"

Moose

Alces alces

Size: 7–10 feet long; 5–6½ feet from the shoulder to the ground; weighs 750–1,200 pounds or more

Habitat: Forested areas, marshes, wetlands, and swamps

Range: They can be found in northeastern New York, as well as in Canada, Alaska, and the northern parts of the eastern US. There are populations in Wyoming, Colorado, and a number of western states.

Food: Leaves, bark, twigs, roots, and aquatic plants

Den: Like other deer, moose dig out beds amid the forest floor.

Young: 1–2 young (calves) that are 25–35 pounds at birth; moose are considered adults at around 2 years old.

Predators: Bears, wolves, and humans

Tracks: Hoofprints are large and heart-shaped.

Moose are a deep brown with a hump on the shoulder and a dewlap (a flap of skin, which is also known as a "bell") hanging down from the throat area. Males are larger than females, and they have large, flat antlers that can be over 4 feet wide and weigh over 30 pounds.

Did you know?

Long-eared bats are skilled fliers! Their long tails and larger wings allow them to skillfully maneuver through the air and hover to catch insects off of plants. They are also known as the whispering bats because their echolocation is so quiet.

Size Comparison Most Active Hibernates

Northern Long-eared Bat

Myotis septentrionalis

Size: 3–3½ inches long; wingspan of 9–10 inches; weighs ⅕–¼ ounces

Habitat: Forest, caves, and mines

Range: They are found throughout most of New York and the eastern United States, to Texas and as far north as southern Canada.

Food: Ants, moths, beetles, and flies

Den: Mate in the fall; females form maternal roost in tree cavities or loose bark. They hibernate in caves and mines.

Young: Usually a single pup is born per female. Pups are born hairless and without the ability to fly. Pups learn to fly in 4–6 weeks.

Predators: Birds of prey, like hawks and owls; sometimes snakes and raccoons

Tracks: Although they are rarely on the ground to leave a track, it would show one thumbprint on the forearms and the hind footprint.

The northern long-eared bat is a medium-size bat with brown to dark-brown fur on their body and brown wings. Their underside is pale brown to tan. They have long ears, a tail, and large wings.

The northern long-eared bat does not often leave tracks.

Did you know?

The raccoon is great at catching fish and other aquatic animals, such as mussels and crawfish. They are also excellent swimmers, but they apparently avoid swimming because the water makes their fur heavy. Raccoons can turn their feet 180 degrees; this helps them when climbing, especially when going headfirst down trees.

Size Comparison   Most Active   Track Size   Hibernates

3"

Northern Raccoon

Procyon lotor

Size: 24–40 inches long; weighs 15–28 pounds

Habitat: Woody areas, grasslands, suburban and urban areas, wetlands, and marshes

Range: They are found throughout New York and the US; they are also found in Mexico and southern Canada.

Food: Eggs, insects, garbage, garden plants, berries, nuts, fish, carrion, small mammals, and aquatic invertebrates like crawfish and mussels

Den: Raccoon dens are built in hollow trees, abandoned burrows, caves, and human-made structures.

Young: 2–6 young (kits) are born around March through July. They are born weighing 2 ounces, are around 4 inches long, and are blind with lightly colored fur.

Predators: Coyotes, foxes, bobcats, humans, and even large birds of prey

Tracks: Their front tracks resemble human handprints. The back tracks sort of look like human footprints.

The northern raccoon has dense fur with variations of brown, black, and white streaks. It has black, mask-like markings on its face and a black-and-gray/brownish ringed tail. During the fall, it will grow a thick layer of fat to stay warm in the winter.

Did you know?

Otters are good swimmers and can close their nostrils while diving. This allows them to dive for as long as 8 minutes and to depths of over 50 feet. Otter fur is the thickest of all mammal fur. River otters have an incredible 67,000 hairs for every square centimeter!

Size Comparison   Most Active   Track Size

3"

Northern River Otter

Lontra canadensis

Size: 29–48 inches long; weighs 10–33 pounds

Habitat: Lakes, marshes, rivers, and large streams; suburban areas

Range: Otters can be found throughout eastern New York and are returning to western New York with the help of humans; they are found across much of the US, except parts of the Southwest and portions of the central US.

Food: Fish, frogs, snakes, crabs, crayfish, mussels, birds, eggs, turtles, and small mammals. They sometimes eat aquatic vegetation too.

Den: They den in burrows along the river, usually under rocks, riverbanks, hollow trees, and vegetation.

Young: 2–4 young (pups) are born between November and May. Pups are born with their eyes closed. They will leave the area at around 6 months old and reach full maturity at around 2 or 3 years.

Predators: Coyotes, bobcats, bears, and dogs

Tracks: Their feet have nonretractable claws and are webbed.

Northern river otters have thick, dark-brown fur and a long, slender body. Their fur is made up of two types: a short under-coat and a coarse top coat that repels water. They have webbed feet and a layer of fat that helps keep them warm in cold water.

Did you know?
The red fox is a great jumper and can leap over 13 feet in one bound. Red foxes are also fast, as they can run up to 30 miles per hour. Red foxes, like wild cats, will hide their food to eat later, often under leaf litter or in holes.

Size Comparison   Most Active   Track Size

2¼"

Red Fox

Vulpes vulpes

Size: 37–42 inches long; weighs 8–15 pounds

Habitat: Grasslands, forest edges, farm fields, and suburban areas

Range: Foxes are common throughout much of New York; they can be found in nearly all of the US, except for the Southwest.

Food: They are omnivores that eat frogs, birds, snakes, small mammals, insects, seeds, nuts, and fruit.

Den: They dig underground dens, sometimes several at once, splitting a litter (babies) between the two. They also use old badger or groundhog holes or tree roots for den sites.

Young: 3–7 young (kits) are born; pups will nurse (drink milk from the mother) for around 10 weeks and will become independent at around 7 months.

Predators: Coyotes, lynx, cougars, and other species of carnivores. Humans trap and hunt foxes for fur.

Tracks: Their footprints resemble dog tracks and have four toe pads; they walk in a line with the hind foot behind the front.

The red fox is a medium-size predator with a burnt orange or rust-like red coat with a bushy, white-tipped tail. The legs are usually black or grayish. The red fox's tail is about one third of its body length.

Did you know?

Skunks help farmers! They save farmers money by feeding on rodents and insects that destroy crops. When skunks spray, they can aim really well! When threatened, a skunk will aim its tail towards the threat and spray a stinky musk into the target's face or eyes.

Size Comparison   Most Active   Track Size 1½"   Hibernates

Striped Skunk

Mephitis mephitis

Size: 17–30 inches long; weighs 6–13 pounds

Habitat: Woodlands, prairies, and suburban areas

Range: Found throughout much of New York; they can be found throughout the US and into Canada and the northern parts of Mexico.

Food: Omnivores (eaters of meat and plants), they eat eggs, fruits, nuts, small mammals, carrion (dead things), insects, amphibians, small reptiles, and even garbage.

Den: Skunks prefer short and shallow natural dens, or dens abandoned by other animals, but will dig dens 3–6 feet long and up to 3 feet deep underground. Dens have multiple hidden entrances, and rooms are usually lined with vegetation.

Young: They have 4–5 young (kits) that are blind at birth; at around 3 weeks they gain vision and the ability to spray.

Predators: Raptors and large carnivores

Tracks: Their front feet have five long, curved claws used for digging; the hind foot also has five toes and is longer and skinnier than the front foot.

The striped skunk is a cat-size, nocturnal (active at night) mammal with black fur and two white stripes that run the entire length of the body. The stripe pattern is usually distinctive to each skunk.

Did you know?

The opossum is the only marsupial native to the US. Marsupials are a special group of animals that are most well-known for their pouches, which they use to carry their young. When frightened, young opossums will play dead (called playing possum) and adults will show their teeth and hiss or run away.

Size Comparison   Most Active   Track Size

Virginia Opossum

Didelphis virginiana

Size: 22–45 inches long; weighs 4–8 pounds

Habitat: Forests, woodlands, meadows, and suburban areas

Range: They are found throughout New York; they are found throughout the eastern US, Canada, and also in Mexico and Costa Rica.

Food: Eggs, small mammals, garbage, insects, worms, birds, fruit, and occasionally small reptiles and amphibians

Den: They den in hollow trees, abandoned animal burrows, and buildings.

Young: A litter of 6–20 young (joeys) are born blind and without fur; their limbs are not fully formed. Young will climb from the birthing area into the mother's pouch and stay until 8 weeks old; they then alternate between the mother's pouch and her back for 4 weeks. At 12 weeks they are independent.

Predators: Hawks, owls, pet cats and dogs, coyotes, and bobcats

Tracks: The front feet are 2 inches long and around 1½ inches wide and resemble a child's hands; the hind feet are 2½ inches long and around 2¼ inches wide; they have fingers in front with a fifth finger that acts as a thumb.

The Virginia opossum has long gray-and-black fur; the face is white, and the tail is pink to gray and furless. Opossums have long claws.

Did you know?

When they first emerge, a deer's antlers are covered in a special skin called velvet. Deer can run up to 40 miles per hour and can jump over 8 feet vertically (high) and over 15 feet horizontally (across).

Size Comparison

Most Active

Track Size
3"

White-tailed Deer

Odocoileus virginianus

Size: 4–6 feet long; 3–4 feet tall at front shoulder; weighs 114–308 pounds

Habitat: Forest edges, brushy fields, woody farmlands, prairies, and swamps

Range: They are found throughout New York and throughout the US, except for much of the Southwest; they are also found in southern Canada and into South America.

Food: Fruits, grasses, tree shrubs, nuts, and bark

Den: Deer do not den but will bed down in tall grasses and shrubby areas.

Young: Deer usually give birth to twins (fawns) that are 3–6 pounds in late May to June. The fawns are born with spots; this coloration helps them hide in vegetation. Young become independent at 1–2 years.

Predators: Wolves, coyotes, bears, bobcats, and humans

Tracks: Both front and hind feet have two teardrop- or comma-shaped toes.

Crepuscular (active at dawn and dusk), white-tailed deer have big brown eyes with eye rings and a long snout with a black, glossy nose. The males have antlers, which fall off each year. All deer have a white tail that they flash upward when alarmed. Deer molt or change fur color twice a year. They sport rusty-brown fur in the summer; in early fall, they transition to winter coats that are grayish brown in color.

Did you know?

The American goldfinch helps restore habitats by spreading seeds. The goldfinch gets its color from a pigment called a carotenoid (say it, cuh-rot-en-oid) in the seeds it eats. It can even feed upside down by using its feet to bring seeds to its mouth.

Nest Type   Most Active

American Goldfinch

Spinus tristis

Size: 4½–5 inches long; wingspan of 9 inches; weighs about half an ounce

Habitat: Grasslands, meadows, suburban areas, and wetlands

Range: Found throughout New York year-round; they can be found throughout much of the United States and southern Canada during various times of the year.

Food: Seeds of plants and trees; sometimes feeds on insects; loves thistle seeds at birdfeeders

Nesting: Goldfinches build a nest in late June.

Nest: Cup-shaped nests are built a couple of feet above-ground out of roots and plant fibers.

Eggs: 2–7 eggs with a bluish-white tint

Young: Young (chicks) hatch around 15 days after being laid; they hatch without feathers and weigh only a gram. Chicks learn to fly after around 11–15 days. Young become mature at around 11 months old.

Predators: Garter snakes, blue jays, American kestrels, and cats

Migration: Nonmigratory in New York; in some states, it will migrate north for breeding territories and south for wintering areas.

During the summer, American goldfinch males are brightly colored with golden-yellow feathers and an orange beak. They have black wings with white wing bars. The crown (top) of the head is black. In winter, they molt, and the males look more like the females. Females are always greenish yellow with hints of yellow around the head.

Did you know?
The American kestrel is the smallest species of falcon not only in the US but in all of North America! It's also the most common falcon of North America.

Nest Type   Most Active

American Kestrel

Falco sparverius

Size: 8½–12¼ inches long; wingspan of 20 inches; weight: 2¾–6 ounces

Habitat: Cities, suburbs, forests, and open areas such as meadows, grasslands, deserts, parks, and farm fields

Range: They can be found throughout most of New York year-round; throughout most of North America except the extreme north of Canada and Alaska.

Food: Grasshoppers, dragonflies, small birds, lizards, and mice; sometimes snakes, bats, and squirrels

Nesting: Nest in cavities that are made by other birds like woodpeckers, in human-made and natural crevices like tree hollows, and in crevices of rock formations.

Nest: They do not use nesting materials but will make a small depression if material is already present.

Eggs: 4–5 yellowish to white or burnt red-brown eggs, 1–1½ inches long and 1 inch wide

Young: Chicks hatch 25–33 days after laying and will leave the nest around 30 days later. Chicks hatch with pink skin and little down feathers.

Predators: Snakes; large birds of prey, like hawks, owls, and crows; bobcats, skunks, and other mammals

Migration: Not a migrant in New York

Kestrels sport a rusty-brown, spotted back. Their tail has a black band that stretches across it. Females have brown-to-reddish wings, and the males have grayish-blue wings. Both males and females have black lines under their eyes that resemble mascara or makeup running down their face.

Did you know?

American robins have a great sense of hearing. They hunt for earthworms underground using only their hearing. Robins are opportunistic feeders in urban (city) areas; they will wait for lawns to be disturbed by mowers, sprinklers, or rain, and then feed on the worms that have emerged.

Nest Type   Most Active

American Robin

Turdus migratorius

Size: 9–11 inches long; wingspan of 17 inches; weighs 2½–3 ounces

Habitat: Cities, forests, and lawns

Range: They can be found throughout New York as year-round residents, and throughout North America except the extreme north of Canada.

Food: Fruits, earthworms, beetle grubs, caterpillars, insects, and grasshoppers

Nesting: April to August

Nest: Cup-shaped nests are exclusively built by the female 5–14 feet off the ground in bushes or trees. Nests are constructed of grass, paper, twigs, and feathers. A new nest is built for each set of eggs.

Eggs: 3–5 sky-blue eggs

Young: Eggs hatch after 14 days of incubation; chicks hatch blind and mostly without feathers. Hatchlings (chicks) leave the nest after 2 weeks but will continue to beg for food from parents.

Predators: Snakes, crows, cats, foxes, raccoons, squirrels, raptors, and weasels

Migration: Do not migrate in New York

American robin males have a dark black-to-gray head with a yellow bill, a brown back, a rusty-orange chest, and a whitish ring around the eyes. Females are similar in color but are not as bright as males, and they usually have a brownish head.

Did you know?

American woodcocks are only found in North America. Males use a courtship dance in the air to attract a mate. They can open the tip of their bill to grab prey. A group of woodcocks is called a plump.

Nest Type   Most Active   Migrates

American Woodcock

Scolopax minor

Size: 9¾–12 inches long; wingspan of 16½–19 inches; weighs 4–9¾ ounces

Habitat: Cities, swamps, forests, lawns, wet thickets, shrub-lands, moist woods, farmlands, and brushy swamps

Range: They can be found throughout New York during the breeding season, and throughout eastern North America, except northern Canada.

Food: They are carnivores that eat earthworms, snails, centipedes, spiders, and some plants and seeds.

Nesting: Early spring

Nest: Ground depression 5 inches wide and 1½ inches deep

Eggs: 1–4 eggs, orange to tannish with brown splotches, each 1½–1¾ inches long and 1¼ inches wide

Young: Chicks hatch 20–22 days after laying. Chicks are pre-cocial at hatching and able to walk and run within a few hours. At 5 weeks, they are independent and leave the nest.

Predators: Snakes, pet dogs and cats, raccoons, skunks, crows, and opossums

Migration: Migrates south in the fall and north in spring

American woodcocks are small, thick-bodied birds with a big head and long bill. They have large, dark-brown eyes and a combination of brown, gray, and black feathers that helps camouflage them with their background. Their big head has three bars across the back. Their face is buff colored; they have a grayish-brown neck with a brown buff-colored breast and stomach area. Females are larger than males.

Did you know?

The bald eagle is an endangered species success story! The bald eagle was once endangered due to a pesticide called DDT that weakened eggshells and caused them to crack early. Through the banning of DDT and other conservation efforts, the bald eagle population recovered, and it was removed from the Endangered Species List in July of 2007.

Nest Type   Most Active   Migrates

Bald Eagle

Haliaeetus leucocephalus

Size: 3½ feet long; wingspan of 6½–8 feet; weighs 8–14 pounds

Habitat: Forests and tree stands (small forests) near river edges, lakes, seashores, and wetlands

Range: They are a resident bird throughout New York; they are found throughout much of the US.

Food: Fish, waterfowl (ducks), rabbits, squirrels, muskrats, and deer carcasses; will steal food from other eagles or ospreys

Nesting: Eagles have lifelong partners that begin nesting in fall, laying eggs November–February.

Nest: They build a large nest out of sticks, high up in trees; the nest can be over 5 feet wide and over 6 feet tall, often shaped like an upside-down cone.

Eggs: 1–3 white eggs

Young: Young (chicks) will hatch at around 35 days; young will leave the nest at around 12 weeks. It takes up to 5 years for eagles to get that iconic look!

Predators: Few; collisions with cars sometimes occur.

Migration: They are short-distance migrators, usually to coastal areas; in New York, many eagles do not migrate at all.

Adult bald eagles have a dark-brown body, a white head and tail, and a golden-yellow beak. Juvenile eagles are mostly brown at first, but their color pattern changes over their first few years. A bald eagle can use its wings as oars to propel itself across bodies of water.

Did you know?

The barred owl has dark-brown eyes; many other owls have yellow eyes. Barred owls, like other owls, have special structures on their primary feathers that allow them to fly silently through the air.

Nest Type

Most Active

Barred Owl

Strix varia

Size: 17–20 inches long; wingspan of 3½ feet; weighs 2 pounds

Habitat: Forested areas, near floodplains of lakes and rivers

Range: They can be found throughout the state of New York; they are found throughout the eastern US and southern Canada, with scattered populations throughout the Pacific Northwest.

Food: Squirrels, rabbits, and mice; will also prey on birds and aquatic animals like frogs, fish, and crayfish

Nesting: Courtship starts in late fall; nesting starts in winter.

Nest: They use hollow trees; they will also use abandoned nests of other animals and human-made nest structures.

Eggs: 2–4 white eggs with a rough shell

Young: Young (chicks) hatch between 27 and 33 days; they have white down feathers and leave the nest around 5 weeks after hatching. They are fully independent at around 6 months and fully mature at around 2 years.

Predators: Great horned owls, raccoons, weasels, and sometimes northern goshawks feed on eggs and young in the nest.

Migration: Barred owls do not migrate.

The barred owl is a medium-size bird with dark rings highlighting the face. Their feathers are brown and grayish, often with streaking or a bar-like pattern. They have no ear tufts and have a rounded head with a yellow beak and brown eyes. They can easily be identified by their call: "Who cooks for you, who cooks for you all?"

Did you know?

Kingfishers inspired human technology! Bullet trains around the world are designed after the kingfisher's beak, which allows it to dive into water without a splash. This design was used in bullet trains to allow them to enter into tunnels without making a large booming sound. This process of modeling human technology after animal features is called biomimicry.

Nest Type   Most Active

Belted Kingfisher

Megaceryle alcyon

Size: 11–13¾ inches long; wingspan is 19–24 inches; weighs 5–6 ounces

Habitat: Forests and grassland areas near rivers, ponds, lakes

Range: Year-round resident that can be found throughout much of New York as well as most of the United States and Canada

Food: Carnivores, they eat mostly fish and other aquatic animals, such as crayfish and frogs, and occasionally other birds, mammals, and berries.

Nesting: Nests are in the form of upward-sloped burrows that are dug in soft banks on or near water. (The upward slopes prevent flooding.)

Nest: Females and males select the nest site together; males do most of the digging.

Eggs: 5–8 white, smooth, glossy eggs are laid per clutch (group of eggs).

Young: Chicks are born featherless with pink skin, closed eyes, and a dark bill. They receive care from both parents. Chicks leave the nest after about 28 days.

Predators: Snakes, hawks, and mammals

Migration: Do not migrate in New York

The belted kingfisher is bluish gray on top; the bottom half is white with a blue/gray belt or band. The wings have white spots on them. Unlike most other birds, the kingfisher female has a different pattern than the male. Females have a second reddish-brown or rusty-orange band on their belly.

Did you know?

Black-capped chickadees have a unique strategy for surviving winter. The area of the brain that aids in memory (the hippocampus) temporarily gets bigger in preparation for winter. This allows them to remember where they hid or cached seeds.

Nest Type   Most Active

Black-capped Chickadee

Poecile atricapillus

Size: 5½–7½ inches long; wingspan of 8 inches; weighs about half an ounce

Habitat: Forests, woodland edges, and suburban and urban areas

Range: They are year-round residents of New York and can be found in the northern United States.

Food: Caterpillars, insects, seeds, spiders, and berries

Nesting: March to August

Nest: Chickadees utilize old woodpecker holes or make their own cup-shaped nests in tree cavities that have been weakened by rot.

Eggs: 4–6 eggs that are white with brown spots

Young: Eggs hatch 12–13 days after they are laid; chicks leave the nest around 15 days after hatching; chickadee parents continue feeding the young for another 5–6 weeks.

Predators: Hawks, owls, shrikes, raccoons, house cats left outside, and other mammals

Migration: They do not migrate.

A black-capped chickadee has a gray body with a black cap, or top of head, and a black throat and beak; they have white cheeks and light bellies.

Did you know?

Bobolinks are the only bird in North America with a white back and black underside. Bobolinks travel over 12,000 miles each year during migration season. They use the Earth's magnetic field and the night sky to migrate.

Nest Type

Most Active

Migrates

Bobolink

Dolichonyx oryzivorus

Size: 6–8½ inches long; wingspan of 10½ inches; weighs 1–2 ounces

Habitat: Overgrown fields, grasslands, prairies, meadows, freshwater marshes, and coastal areas

Range: Breeding resident of New York, the northern US, and southern Canada; migrating resident of the mid-Atlantic to eastern US; overwinters in the southern interior of South America

Food: Weeds, seeds, and other small grains; insects and spiders, rice, oats, and corn

Nesting: May to June

Nest: Female makes nest frame out of grasses and stems and uses fine vegetation to line the inside. Nests are built on the ground.

Eggs: 3–7 pale blue-gray to reddish-brown eggs, with unorganized spots of purple and brown. Eggs are under an inch long and wide.

Young: Chicks hatch 11–14 days after laying with eyes closed and naked besides a sparse cover of yellow down feathers.

Predators: Snakes, raccoons, birds of prey, pet cats, and striped skunks

Migration: Travels to South America during fall and return north in the spring

Male bobolinks have a breeding plumage of a majority black body with a white back and rump. The nape, or back of the neck area, is buffy yellow. Females and nonbreeding males are dull yellowish brown with streaks of dark brown on the back and sides. They have brown stripes on the head and a pink bill.

71

Did you know?

Canada geese sometimes travel over 600 miles in a day. They fly in a V formation, which allows them to travel long distances without stopping because they can switch positions. As the lead bird gets tired, it drops to the back of the line and a new bird leads. The V formation helps them communicate and helps prevent collisions.

Nest Type

Most Active

Canada Goose

Branta canadensis

Size: 2–3½ feet long; wingspan of 5–6 feet; weighs 6½–20 pounds

Habitat: Ponds, marshes, lakes, parks, and farm fields

Range: They can be found throughout New York as residents; they are widespread in the rest of the US.

Food: Omnivores, they eat grasses, aquatic insects, seeds, and some crops, like corn or alfalfa.

Nesting: March to April

Nest: Nests are made on the ground, on elevated areas near the water, or sometimes on a muskrat mound. Nest sites are picked with protection in mind; areas that have clear views and vantage points are more likely to be used.

Eggs: 2–8 cream-colored eggs that are 3 inches long and about 2½ inches wide

Young: Goslings hatch about a month after being laid. They are born with yellow down feathers that they lose as they get older. At the time of hatching, they can swim and walk.

Predators: Mink, raccoons, foxes, dogs, and great horned owls

Migration: Do not migrate in New York

The Canada goose is recognizable by its famous honk and body pattern of brown feathers with a black neck, head, bill, and even feet. They have white cheek feathers.

Did you know?
Because of the way their legs are situated on their body, loons aren't good at walking on land. Loons have to get a running (or swimming) start to take off from the water.

Nest Type   Most Active   Migrates

Common Loon

Gavia immer

Size: 28–36 inches long; wingspan of 40–55 inches; weighs 3½–13 pounds

Habitat: Quiet freshwater lakes and coastal waters

Range: Found throughout northern New York during breeding season and southern parts of New York as migrants; they're found in several other northern states and in Canada during the breeding season, and they're widespread across the US during migration.

Food: Fish, snails, and crayfish

Nesting: May to August

Nest: The male selects the nesting spot; males and females will build a nest out of grasses and reeds together near the water.

Eggs: 2 eggs that have a brown base layer with brown spots

Young: Young (adorably called loonlets) usually hatch in 29 days, covered with dark, fuzzy down; they can swim immediately after hatching. Chicks will ride on a parent's back.

Predators: Mink, raccoons, skunks, other loons, and eagles

Migration: New York loons migrate to the Atlantic Coast, the Gulf of Mexico, and the Florida coast, depending on where they are located.

The common loon sports a black-and-white checkered back and a dark green-and-blackish head with red eyes and a black bill. During the fall, adults change a great deal: they lose their checkered spots, the head feathers become gray, and the bill lightens to a dull gray.

Did you know?

The double-crested cormorant does not have oil glands like other aquatic birds; this is why you will see it on a rock or a post with its wings spread: it's drying itself off. The cormorant's bill curves at the end, perfect for grasping fish and other prey.

Nest Type   Most Active   Migrates

Double-crested Cormorant

Nannopterum auritum

Size: 26–35 inches long; wingspan of 45–48½ inches; weighs 2½–3 pounds

Habitat: Freshwater lakes, rivers, swamps, coastal waters

Range: They can be found across North America. In New York, they can be found statewide.

Food: They are carnivores that eat fish, insects, snails, and crayfish.

Nesting: April to August; male chooses the nest site before finding a female. Nest in groups with other water birds

Nest: Veteran parents may repair an old nest. Otherwise, they build a new nest on the ground or in a tree. Nests are made of sticks and lined with grass. Nests can be as wide as 3 feet and over 1½ feet tall.

Eggs: On average, 4 light-bluish-white eggs are laid at a time.

Young: Young chicks (shaglets) usually hatch in 25–28 days; they can swim immediately after hatching.

Predators: Eggs are vulnerable to raccoons, gulls, jays, foxes, and coyotes. Adults and chicks are preyed on by coyotes, foxes, raccoons, eagles, and great horned owls.

Migration: Northern populations migrate south in winter.

Adults have black feathers and topaz-colored eyes, with an orange bill, throat, and face area; they have black feet that are webbed like a duck's. The tail is short. During breeding season, adults may have a "double crest" of black feathers or sometimes white, depending on the location. This is where they get the name double-crested cormorant. Young are all brown or black.

Did you know?

Bluebirds are not really blue! The "blue" that we see is visible because of the way that light hits the structure of the feathers, but there is no blue pigment in their feathers. The eastern bluebird will use a large variety of sounds to attract a mate; sometimes, an individual male will sing many different songs per minute!

Nest Type

Most Active

Migrates

Eastern Bluebird

Sialia sialis

Size: 7 inches long; wingspan of 13 inches; weighs 1 ounce

Habitat: Open woodlands, meadows, prairies, gardens, parks, and suburban areas

Range: They can be found statewide in New York and throughout the eastern and southern United States.

Food: Berries, insects, and seeds

Nesting: Late March to late July or early August

Nest: Bluebirds utilize woodpecker cavities and other tree holes, as well as nesting boxes. The nest is lined with grasses.

Eggs: Clutch (group of eggs) size is 3–6; eggs are a light blue color.

Young: Chicks hatch mostly featherless and blind. They gain sight in 1 week and have all feathers at around 2 weeks. Chicks will leave the nest at around 3 weeks but will receive care until about 4 weeks.

Predators: House sparrows and European starlings will invade nests and destroy eggs. Eggs and young are preyed upon by house cats, raccoons, rodents, and more.

Migration: They migrate to the southern United States.

Eastern bluebird males are a rich blue with a rusty breast; females are a dull brown with faint blue feathers. Bluebirds are known to return to New York in early to mid-March.

Did you know?

Eastern and western meadowlarks look almost exactly the same. A few ways to tell them apart are that the western meadowlark is a little less vibrant in color and has a different song. The western meadowlark can also be found in groups or flocks more often than the eastern.

Nest Type

Most Active

Migrates

Eastern Meadowlark

Sturnella magna

Size: 7½–10 inches long; wingspan of 14–16 inches; weighs 3–5 ounces

Habitat: Farm fields, grasslands, and wet fields

Range: Found throughout New York during the breeding season. The eastern meadowlark can be found from the Atlantic as far west as Minnesota and parts of Arizona and Nebraska, where the range overlaps with the western meadowlark.

Food: Mostly insects and other soft-bodied invertebrates

Nesting: Males select a territory in March. When females arrive a couple of weeks later, they select a mate after going through an air courtship display.

Nest: Female builds a cup-shaped depression in the ground.

Eggs: 3–5 white eggs with purple and brown spots. Eggs are 1 inch long and just under an inch wide.

Young: Female birds incubate the eggs for 13–16 days; chicks hatch with eyes closed and naked, with pink-orange skin and a few gray down feathers present. They receive care from both parents and will fledge (leave) the nest around 10 days or so.

Predators: Pet cats, foxes, dogs, skunks, falcons, coyotes, hawks, and occasionally owls

Migration: In fall, they migrate south; they return in spring.

Meadowlarks have a striped brown head and upper half, and a gray bill. They have a yellow underside with their breast adorned with a black "V." Their tail feathers have thick bars.

Did you know?

The great blue heron is the largest and most common heron species in New York. A heron's eye color changes as it ages. The eyes start out gray but transition to yellow over time. Great blue herons swallow their prey whole.

Nest Type

Most Active

Migrates

Great Blue Heron

Ardea herodias

Size: 3–4½ feet long; wingspan of 6–7 feet; weighs 5–7 pounds

Habitat: Lakes, ponds, rivers, marshes, lagoons, wetlands, and coastal areas like beaches

Range: They can be found throughout New York, as well as the entire United States and down into Mexico.

Food: Fish, rats, crabs, shrimp, grasshoppers, crayfish, other birds, small mammals, snakes, and lizards

Nesting: May to August

Nest: 2–3 feet across and saucer shaped; often grouped in large rookeries (colonies) in tall trees along the water's edge. Nests are built out of sticks and are often located in dead trees more than 100 feet above the ground; nests are used year after year.

Eggs: 3–7 pale bluish eggs

Young: Chicks will hatch after 28 days of incubation; young will stay in the nest for around 10 weeks. They reach reproductive maturity at just under 2 years.

Predators: Eagles, crows, gulls, raccoons, bears, and hawks

Migration: Many migrate, especially in northern New York

The great blue heron is a large wading bird with blue and gray upper body feathers; the belly area is white. They have long yellow legs that they use to stalk prey in the water. Great blue herons are famous for stalking prey at the water's edge; their specially adapted feet keep them from sinking into the mud!

Did you know?

A great horned owl can exert a crushing force of over 300 pounds with its talons. Despite its name, the great horned owl doesn't have horns at all. Instead, the obvious tufts on its head are made of feathers. Scientists aren't sure exactly how the tufts function, but they may help them stay hidden.

Nest Type   Most Active

Great Horned Owl
Bubo virginianus

Size: Up to 23 inches long; wingspan of 45 inches; weighs 3 pounds

Habitat: Woods; swamps; desert edges; as well as heavily populated areas such as cities, suburbs, and parks

Range: They are found throughout New York and the continent of North America.

Food: They eat a variety of foods, but mostly mammals. Sometimes they eat other birds as well.

Nesting: They have lifelong partnerships, with nesting season starting in early winter; egg-laying starts in mid-January to February.

Nest: Nests are found 20–50 feet off the ground. They tend to reuse nests from other raptors or hollowed-out trees.

Eggs: The female lays 2–4 whitish eggs. Eggs are incubated for around 30 days.

Young: Young can fly at around 9 weeks old. The parents care for and feed young for several months.

Predators: Young owls are preyed upon by foxes, coyotes, bears, and opossums. As adults, they are rarely attacked by other birds of prey, such as golden eagles and goshawks.

Migration: Great horned owls are not regular migrators, but some individuals will travel south during the winter.

They are bulky birds with large ear tufts, a rusty brown-to-grayish face with a black border, and large bright eyes. The body color tends to be brown; the wing pattern is checkered with an intermingled dark brown. The chest and belly areas are light brown and have white bars.

Did you know?

Downy woodpeckers are the smallest woodpecker species in North America. Hairy woodpeckers can hear insects traveling under the tree bark. Downy woodpeckers have a built-in mask, or special feathers, near their nostrils that helps them to avoid breathing in wood chips while pecking.

Nest Type   Most Active

Hairy/Downy Woodpecker

Leuconotopicus villosus/Dryobates pubescens

Size: Hairy: 7–10 inches long; wingspan of 13–16 inches; weighs 3 ounces. Downy: 5½–7 inches long; wingspan of 10–12 inches; weighs less than an ounce

Habitat: Forested areas, parks, woodlands, and orchards

Range: Throughout New York and across the United States

Food: Hairy: beetles, ants, caterpillars, fruits, and seeds. Downy: beetles, ants, galls, wasps, seeds, and berries

Nesting: Hairy: April to July. Downy: April to July

Nest: In both woodpecker species, pairs will work together to create a cavity. Both parents also help to incubate eggs.

Eggs: Hairy: 3–7 white eggs. Downy: 3–8 white eggs

Young: Hairy woodpeckers' eggs will hatch 2 weeks after being laid and then fledge (develop enough feathers to fly) after another month. Downy woodpeckers' eggs will hatch after about 12 days and fledge 18–21 days after hatching. Both species hatch blind and featherless.

Predators: American kestrels, snakes, sharp-shinned hawks, pet cats, rats, squirrels, and Cooper's hawks

Migration: Woodpeckers are year-round residents.

Hairy woodpeckers and downy woodpeckers look strikingly similar with their color pattern. One way to distinguish them is to look at the size of the body and bill. The downy woodpecker is smaller than the hairy woodpecker and has a shorter bill. If you look at the tail feathers of the two species, you will also see that the hairy woodpecker does not have black spots, while the downy's tail does.

Did you know?

Groups of hooded merganser ducklings will avoid being attacked by raptors by mimicking the shape of a swimming muskrat. The merganser is one of the few duck species in our area that eats lots of fish; it can dive underwater for up to two minutes while fishing.

Nest Type   Most Active   Migrates

Hooded Merganser

Lophodytes cucullatus

Size: Up to 1½ feet long; wingspan of 2 feet; weighs 1–2 pounds

Habitat: Wooded lakes and streams, marshes, small rivers, and woodlands adjacent to bodies of water

Range: They can be found throughout the state of New York as year-round residents. Several populations can be found across the United States and Canada.

Food: Fish, tadpoles, aquatic insects, and crustaceans

Nesting: April to June

Nest: Nests are shallow, bowl shaped, and made inside tree cavities or human-made wooden duck-nesting structures. Down feathers and wood chips are added to the cavity.

Eggs: 10–12 white eggs

Young: After a month of incubation, eggs will hatch, and ducklings will leave the nest within 24 hours of hatching. They can fly after about 65 days.

Predators: Hawks, humans, snakes, mink, and martens

Migration: Populations migrate south for the winter, while others will migrate north and overwinter on the Great Lakes.

Hooded merganser males have a black-and-white crest that can help distinguish them from females. Other identifying features include brilliant yellow eyes, black-and-white feathers on its breast and back, and a brown side. The females are duller with a brown crest on the back of the head, brown feathers, and brown eyes.

Did you know?

When viewed straight-on, the yellow portion on the mallard's bill resembles a cartoon dog's head. Most domesticated ducks share the mallard as their ancestor. Mallard feathers are waterproof; they use oil from the preen gland beneath their feathers to help aid in repelling water. Mallards are the most common duck in the United States and New York.

Nest Type   Most Active

Mallard
Anas platyrhynchos

Size: 24 inches long; wingspan of 36 inches; weighs 2½–3 pounds

Habitat: Lakes, ponds, rivers, and marshes

Range: They are found throughout New York; the population stretches across the United States and Canada into Mexico and as far up as central Alaska.

Food: Insects, worms, snails, aquatic vegetation, sedge seeds, grasses, and wild rice

Nesting: April to August

Nest: The nest is constructed on the ground, usually near a body of water.

Eggs: 9–13 eggs

Young: Eggs hatch 26–28 days after being laid. The ducklings are fully feathered and have the ability to swim at the time of hatching. Ducklings are cared for until they're 2–3 months old and reach reproductive maturity at 1 year old.

Predators: Humans, crows, mink, coyotes, raccoons, and snapping turtles

Migration: Year-round resident

Male mallards are gray with an iridescent green head with a tinge of purple spotting, a white line along the collar, rusty-brown chest, yellow bill, and orange legs and feet. Females are dull brown with a yellow bill, a bluish area near the tail, and orange feet.

Did you know?

A mourning dove eats around 12% or more of its body weight each day. Mourning doves will store seeds and grain in their crop (pouch on their neck). Some people mistake the mourning dove call for an owl call.

Nest Type

Most Active

Mourning Dove

Zenaida macroura

Size: 8–14 inches long; wingspan of 17–19 inches; weighs 3½–6 ounces

Habitat: Woodlands, parks, grasslands, scrub areas, farm fields, and suburban and urban areas

Range: In New York, it can be found throughout the state; it is abundant throughout southern Canada and the continental United States.

Food: Fruits, insects, and seeds; young feed on crop milk

Nesting: Courtship begins in April.

Nest: Males will show females several potential nesting sites. The female will choose the site, the male will bring nest-building materials to the female, and she will then construct the nest.

Eggs: 2 white eggs, incubated by both parents

Young: Within 2 weeks, hatchlings will depart the nest, but they receive care for another week or so.

Predators: Cats, falcons, hawks, raccoons, and humans

Migration: Year-round resident

Mourning doves are gray and brown. They have a brown chest and pointed tail that has a white tip on it. Their beak is gray-ish-black, the eyes are black, and on their head just below the eyes they have a black spot. They can be recognized by their spooky "hoo, hoo, hoo" call or the whistling of their wings when they take off.

Did you know?

Cardinals are very territorial and will sometimes attack their own reflection thinking that another cardinal has entered its territory. The early bird gets the worm, and cardinals are some of the first birds active in the morning.

Nest Type   Most Active

Northern Cardinal

Cardinalis cardinalis

Size: 8–9 inches long; wingspan of 12 inches

Habitat: Hardwood forests, urban areas, orchards, backyards, and fields

Range: They are found throughout New York, as well as the eastern and midwestern parts of the United States.

Food: Seeds, fruits, insects, spiders, and centipedes

Nesting: March to August

Nest: The cup-shaped nest is built by females in thick foliage, usually at least 1 foot off the ground. It can be 3 inches tall and 4 inches wide.

Eggs: The female lays 2–5 off-white eggs with a variety of colored speckles.

Young: About 2 weeks after eggs are laid, chicks hatch with their eyes closed and mostly naked, aside from sparsely placed down feathers.

Predators: Hawks, owls, and squirrels

Migration: Cardinals do not migrate.

Northern cardinal males are bright-red birds with a black face. Females are a washed-out red or brown. Both males and females have a crest (tuft of feathers on the head), an orange beak, and grayish legs. Cardinals can be identified by their laser-gun-like call.

Did you know?

The osprey is nicknamed the "fish hawk" because it is the only hawk in North America that mainly eats live fish. An osprey will rotate its catch to put it in line with its body, pointing headfirst, which allows for less resistance in flight as the air travels over the fish.

Nest Type   Most Active   Migrates

Osprey

Pandion haliaetus

Size: 21–23 inches long; wingspan of 59–71 inches; weighs 3–4½ pounds

Habitat: Near lakes, ponds, rivers, swamps, and reservoirs

Range: Found in New York during the breeding and migration seasons, and throughout the US and Canada and Alaska

Food: Feeds mostly on fish; they sometimes eat mammals, birds, and reptiles if there are few fish.

Nesting: For ospreys that migrate, egg-laying happens in April and May. The female will take on most of the incubation of the eggs, as well as the jobs of keeping the offspring warm and providing protection.

Nest: Platform nests are constructed out of twigs and sticks. Nests are constructed on trees, snags, or human-made objects like cellular towers and telephone poles.

Eggs: The mother lays 1–3 cream-colored eggs; they have splotches of various shades of brown and pinkish red on them.

Young: Chicks hatch after around 36 days and have brown-and-white down feathers. Ospreys fledge around 50–55 days after hatching and will receive care from parents for another 2 months or so.

Predators: Owls, eagles, foxes, skunks, raccoons, and snakes

Migration: Ospreys migrate south to wintering areas in the fall.

Ospreys are raptors, and they have a brown upper body and white lower body. The wings are brown on the outside and white on the underside, with brown spotting and streaks toward the edge. The head is white with a brown band that goes through the eye area, highlighting the yellow eyes.

Did you know?

The peregrine falcon is the fastest diving bird in the world. A peregrine falcon can reach speeds over 200 miles per hour (mph) when diving. To aid in diving and maneuvering in the air, like most other birds, peregrine falcons have a third eyelid called a nictitating membrane that helps to keep out debris and wind.

Most Active

Migrates

Peregrine Falcon

Falco peregrinus

Size: 14–19½ inches long; wingspan of 39–43 inches; weighs 1–3½ pounds

Habitat: Hardwood forests, coastal areas and marshes, urban areas, orchards, backyards, and fields

Range: They are found throughout the US and much of New York during migration.

Food: Carnivores, they feed on pigeons, songbirds, aquatic birds, rodents, and sometimes bats

Nesting: February to March. Pairs mate for life and reuse nests. The female chooses a nest site and will scrape a shallow hole in loose soil or sand. Nests are usually on cliff edges or tall buildings. Sometimes they even use abandoned nests of other large birds.

Nest: Shallow ground scrapes about 8–9 inches wide and 2 inches deep with no extra nesting materials added

Eggs: 3–5 off-white-to-brown eggs speckled brown or purple

Young: 30 days after eggs are laid, chicks (or eyas) will hatch with eyes closed and covered in off-white down.

Predators: Great horned owls, golden eagles, and humans

Migration: Northern and central populations migrate for breeding. Coastal populations are less likely to migrate.

The female is slightly larger than the male. Peregrine falcons have gray wings with black-to-gray, bar-like marks and deep-black wing tips. The breast and belly areas are covered with black-to-brown horizontal streaks or bars. They have a black head and black marks below the eyes. The neck is white. The beak, legs, eye rings, and feet are yellow.

Did you know?

The red-tailed hawk is the most abundant hawk in North America. (Look for it on power lines!) The red-tailed hawk's scream is the sound effect that you hear when soaring eagles are shown in movies. Eagles do not screech like hawks, so filmmakers use hawk calls instead!

Nest Type

Most Active

Migrates

Red-tailed Hawk (RT)/
Red-shouldered Hawk (RS)

Buteo jamaicensis / Buteo lineatus

Size: RT: 19–25 inches long; wingspan of 47–57 inches; weighs 2½–4 pounds. RS: 16½–24 inches long; wingspan of 37–43 inches; weighs around 1 pound

Habitat: RT: Deserts, woodlands, fields. RS: Forests, swamps, grasslands, urban areas

Range: RT: Year-round in southern New York, and breeding resident in northern parts and throughout North America. RS: Breeding resident throughout most of the state, and year-round in southeastern New York, eastern US, and parts of the Pacific Coast.

Food: RT: Rodents, birds, reptiles, bats, and insects. RS: Small mammals, lizards, snakes, crayfish, songbirds

Nesting: Hawks mate for life; nesting starts in March.

Nest: RT: Both parents build a large cup-shaped nest made of sticks and branches. RS: Both male and female build a cup-shaped nest 20 feet off the ground.

Eggs: RT: White with colored blotches. RS: Off-white or slightly blue with varied markings

Young: RT: Young hatch after 30 days. They can fly at 5–6 weeks. RS: Chicks can fly after 5–6 weeks.

Predators: RT: Owls and crows. RS: Snakes, mammals, and owls

Migration: Birds in the northern areas will migrate short distances, while those in the southern part do not migrate.

Red-tailed hawks are named for their rusty-red tails! They have brown heads and a creamy, light-brown chest with a band of brown streaking. Red-shouldered hawks have a reddish-brown head and back, with rusty undersides with white barring. **101**

Did you know?

Red-winged blackbirds are one of the most abundant songbirds in the United States. Sometimes their winter roost (colony) can have several thousand to up to a million birds. In many areas, red-winged blackbirds are considered a pest because of their love of grain and seeds from farm fields. In others, they are welcomed because they eat insects that are considered pests to farmers.

Nest Type

Most Active

Red-winged Blackbird

Agelaius phoeniceus

Size: 7–9½ inches long; wingspan of 13 inches; weighs 2 ounces

Habitat: Marshes, lakeshores, meadows, parks, and open fields

Range: Year-round residents across New York; ranges from central Canada through the US and into Mexico

Food: Dragonflies, spiders, beetles, snails, seeds, and fruits

Nesting: February to August

Nest: Female builds a cup from plant material.

Eggs: 3–4 eggs that come in a variety of colors, from pale blue to gray with black-and-brown spots or streaks

Young: Chicks hatch blind and naked after around 12 days of incubation. Hatchlings will leave the nest after 12 days but will continue to receive care for another 5 weeks.

Predators: Raccoons, mink, owls, and raptors

Migration: Year-round residents that do not migrate

Red-winged blackbird males are a sleek black with an orangish-red spot that overlays a dandelion-yellow spot on the wings. Females have a combination of dark-brown and light-brown streaks throughout the body. Male red-winged blackbirds spend much of breeding season defending their territory from other males and attacking predators or anything else that gets too close to the nest.

Did you know?

Short-eared owls make their nests on the ground. Males will use wing claps to attract mates during a courtship display.

Nest Type

Most Active

Migrates

Short-eared owl

Asio flammeus

Size: 13½–17 inches long; wingspan of 33½–40½ inches; weighs 7¼–16¾ ounces

Habitat: Grasslands, rock quarries, savannas, marshes, dunes, gravel pits, thickets, and coastal grasslands

Range: Seen throughout New York in the winter and a year-round resident in northern New York, as well as much of the US.

Food: Mice, voles, shrews, moles, lemmings, rabbits, pocket gophers, bats, rats, weasels, and birds

Nesting: March to June

Nest: Ground-scraped bowl is made by female and lined with grasses and down feathers. Nests are usually built on ridges or hummocks where vegetation can hide them.

Eggs: 4–7 creamy-white eggs, 1½–1¾ inches long and 1½ inches wide

Young: Chicks are hatched 21–37 days after laying with eyes closed and downy feathers. They will fledge 12–18 days after hatching and fly within another 9–10 days.

Predators: Ravens and crows, dogs, skunks, foxes, and coyotes

Migration: Some owls migrate north to breeding areas, while others are year-round residents.

Short-eared owls have short tufts of feathers, rounded heads, and are medium-size. They have a pale-to-white face with yellow eyes that are outlined in black. They have broad wings and a short tail. Their body is brown with spots of white, and they have a pale chest with streaks of brown.

Did you know?

Snowy owls are one of the few species of owls that are diurnal, which means they hunt during the daytime, while most of the other owls hunt at night. Snowy owls can hunt over 1,500 lemmings (small rodents related to voles) in a single year. Because of their thick feathers, snowy owls are the largest owls in North America by weight.

Nest Type   Most Active   Migrates

Snowy Owl

Bubo scandiacus

Size: 20½–28 inches; wingspan of 49½–57 inches; weighs 56½–104 ounces

Habitat: Prairies, fields, marshes, farmland

Range: During the winter, they can be found throughout the state of New York; they can also be found throughout New England and westward to Washington state.

Food: Small mammals, especially lemmings (a rodent). They also eat birds.

Nesting: Snowy owls usually breed during the months of May and September. Males court females using a mix of displays, one performed while in the air and the other performed while on the ground.

Nest: Female builds the nest by hollowing out an area on the ground and using her body to make the nest shape.

Eggs: Usually 3–11 white eggs, about 2 inches long and wide, are laid per brood.

Young: Chicks or owlets hatch blind with downy feathers 30 days after laying. Chicks receive care from both parents. After about 14–25 days, chicks will venture out from the nest.

Predators: Foxes, wolves, dogs, and humans

Migration: They migrate south from extreme northern Canada and Alaska to interior and southern Canada and the northern US during the winter.

Snowy owls are white with brown bars and spots. The males are a more brilliant and vibrant white, while the females are darker in color with more spots and bars than the males. Both males and females have bright-yellow eyes.

Did you know?

The trumpeter swan is the largest and heaviest waterfowl species found in North America. Trumpeter swans will use their webbed feet to aid in egg incubation. When feeding on deep aquatic plants, they will create a current in the water by pumping their feet; this current allows them to pull aquatic plants from the bottom more easily.

Nest Type

Most Active

Migrates

Trumpeter Swan

Cygnus buccinator

Size: 60–72 inches long; wingspan of 72–84 inches; weighs 17–28 pounds

Habitat: Lakes, rivers, marshes, wetlands, and coastal areas

Range: They are found in isolated populations where New York borders the Great Lakes and in surrounding areas. They can also be found in isolated populations throughout the northern United States and Canada.

Food: Aquatic plants, small fish, crustaceans, and fish eggs

Nesting: April to June

Nest: Both male and female swans construct the circular nest. Nest-building can take 2–5 weeks to complete.

Eggs: 4–6 cream or white eggs

Young: Young hatch 32–37 days after eggs are laid; they leave the nest after a day and can fly after around 100 days. They are independent at around 10 months and reach full maturity between 4 and 7 years.

Predators: Eagles, owls, coyotes, mink, otters, and ravens

Migration: Northern populations will move south in winter to areas with open water.

Adult trumpeter swans are large white birds with long necks, black bills, and webbed feet; juveniles (young) are a grayish color. Trumpeter swans are only found in North America. They have a thick layer of down feathers that aid in living in cold areas.

Did you know?

Turkeys sometimes fly at night, unlike most birds, and land in trees to roost. Turkeys have some interesting facial features; the red skin growth on a turkey's face above the beak is called a snood, while the growth under the beak is called a wattle. Wild turkeys can have more than 5,000 feathers.

Nest Type

Most Active

Wild Turkey

Meleagris gallopavo

Size: 3–4 feet long; wingspan of 5 feet; males weigh 16–25 pounds; females weigh 9–11 pounds.

Habitat: Woodlands and grasslands

Range: Found throughout New York. They also can be found in the eastern US and have been introduced in many western areas of the country.

Food: Grain, snakes, frogs, insects, acorns, berries, and ferns

Nesting: April to September

Nest: The nest is built on the ground using leaves as bedding, in brush or near the base of trees or fallen logs.

Eggs: 10–12 tan eggs with very small reddish-brown spots

Young: Poults (young) hatch about a month after eggs are laid; they will flock with the mother for a year. When young are still unable to fly, the mom will stay on the ground with her poults to provide protection and warmth. When poults grow up, they are known as hens if they are female, or as gobblers or toms if they are male.

Predators: Humans, foxes, raccoons, owls, eagles, skunks

Migration: Turkeys do not migrate.

A wild turkey is a large bird that is dark brown and black with some iridescent feathers. Males will fan out their tail to attract a mate. When threatened, they will also fan out their tail and rush the predator, sometimes kicking and puncturing prey with the spurs on their feet.

Did you know?

Wood ducks will "mimic" a soccer player when a predator is near their young: they flop! Female wood ducks will fake a broken wing to lure predators away from their young. Wood duck hatchlings must jump from the nest after hatching to reach the water. They can jump 50 feet or more without hurting themselves.

Nest Type

Most Active

Migrates

Wood Duck

Aix sponsa

Size: 15–20 inches long; wingspan of 30 inches; weighs about 1 pound

Habitat: Swamps, woody ponds, and marshes

Range: They are year-long residents throughout New York, except for the northern part of the state, where they are breeding residents. They are also found in the eastern US, southern Mexico, the Pacific Northwest, and on the West Coast.

Food: Fruits; nuts; and aquatic vegetation, especially duckweed, sedges, and grasses

Nesting: March to August

Nest: Wood ducks use hollow trees, abandoned woodpecker cavities, and human-made nesting boxes.

Eggs: 8–15 off-white eggs are laid once a year. Sometimes females will lay eggs in another female's nest; this process is called egg dumping.

Young: Eggs hatch about a month after being laid. Chicks will leave the nest after a day and fly within 8 weeks.

Predators: Raccoons, mink, fish, hawks, snapping turtles, owls, humans, and muskrats

Migration: They are year-round residents in much of New York; breeding residents migrate southward during the fall.

Wood duck males have a brightly colored crest (tuft of feathers) of iridescent (shimmering) green, red, and purple, with a mahogany (brown) upper breast area and tan bottom. Males also have red eyes. Females are brown to gray. Wood ducks have strong claws that enable them to climb up trees into cavities.

Did you know?

The American toad is the most commonly observed toad in New York. While the American toad has warts on it, you cannot get warts from touching it. Toads are toxic (but not to humans); they have two parotid glands—one behind each eye that produces a toxin they release to prevent predators from eating them.

Most Active 　　Hibernates

American Toad

Anaxyrus americanus

Size: 2–4 inches long; weighs 1½–2 ounces

Habitat: Prairies, forests, suburban areas, swamps, and other wetlands

Range: They are found throughout New York and from New England south into parts of Mississippi, Alabama, and Georgia.

Food: Insects, worms, snails, ants, moths, and beetles

Mating: February to July

Nest: No nest

Eggs: 2,000–19,000 or more eggs are laid in bodies of water attached to vegetation or the bottom of shallow water.

Young: Eggs hatch 3–10 days after laying. They will stay in the tadpole stage 40–65 days. It takes 2–3 years to reach reproductive maturity.

Predators: Hognoses and other snakes, raccoons, and birds; as tadpoles: beetles, crayfish, birds, and dragonfly larvae

The American toad has a brown-to-clay-red-colored base layer with brown and black spots and noticeable warts on its body. During the summer or extreme heat, toads can reduce their metabolic rate and cool themselves down.

Did you know?

Bog turtles are the smallest species of turtle in North America. Bog turtles' shells are not strong enough to protect them from predators, so they will bury themselves into mud when threatened.

Most Active   Hibernates

Bog Turtle

Glyptemys muhlenbergii

Size: 3–4½ inches long; weighs 4 ounces

Habitat: Meadows, prairies, forests, suburban areas, bogs, marshes, swamps, and other wetlands

Range: Found as far north as New York and as far south as northeast Georgia and westward to Ohio. In New York, they can be found in western parts surrounding the Great Lakes and in the southeastern parts of the state.

Food: Omnivore that eats aquatic plants, algae, insects, snails, earthworms, seeds, berries, snakes, and carrion or dead animals

Mating: April–June

Nest: Nests are built in elevated portions of grasses or moss in wetlands; females dig a cavity.

Eggs: 2–5, white, elongated eggs, about 1¼ inches long

Young: Young hatch 42–70 days after laying; temperature determines the sex of hatchlings. Hatchlings are just under an inch. Males are larger than females at hatching and grow faster; both sexes are fully grown around 5–6 years but are not reproductively mature until 8–11 years.

Predators: Raccoons, skunks, foxes, dogs, and birds

Bog turtles have a dome-shaped carapace (top shell) that comes in variations of light–dark brown. The carapace has rings on its scutes that usually have orange-yellow centers. The plastron is also varying shades of brown. They have dark-brown-to-black skin with a large yellow-to-orange or reddish spot on the side of their neck. Males have a shell that caves inward, while females have a relatively flat shell.

Did you know?

Eastern box turtles help to spread various species of plants. As omnivores, they will eat different types of berries, and as they move to other locations, they expel the seeds in their waste, creating new plants when those seeds grow. They have the ability to bring their limbs and head under their shell and shut themselves inside.

Most Active   Hibernates

Eastern Box Turtle

Terrapene carolina carolina

Size: 5–6 inches long; weighs 5–5½ ounces

Habitat: Forests, open grasslands, pastures, shrublands, wetlands, farm fields

Range: Can be found as far north as Maine, as far south as Florida, and as far west as Texas. In New York, it can be found in the southeast region of the state.

Food: Omnivores; earthworms, slugs, grasses, berries, mushrooms, and carrion

Mating: Late spring–early autumn

Nest: Shallow nest built in loose material (dirt, soil, sandy clay)

Eggs: 1–9 eggs

Young: Hatchlings hatch 50–70 days after laying and will reach reproductive maturity at around 5 years old.

Predators: Crows, ravens, hawks, owls, raccoons, foxes, and squirrels

Eastern box turtles have sharp beaks, thick limbs, and a dome-shaped carapace (top of shell). The carapace is brownish to black and has various patterns of orange and yellowish spots. The skin is dark brown to yellowish tan with orange, yellow, and red spots. Males have bluish spots on their cheeks, legs, and throat. Males also have red irises, while the females have brown.

Did you know?

Eastern garter snakes are highly social and will form groups with other snakes and often other species to overwinter together in a burrow or hole. When threatened by a predator or handled, they will sometimes musk or emit a foul-smelling, oily substance from their cloaca (butt).

Most Active   Hibernates

Eastern Garter Snake

Thamnophis sirtalis

Size: 14–36 inches long (rarely over 17 inches); weighs 5–5½ ounces

Habitat: Forests and forest edges, grasslands, and suburban areas

Range: They are found throughout New York and can be found in the eastern US from Minnesota, southward to eastern Texas, and then east towards the Atlantic coast.

Food: Frogs, snails, toads, salamanders, insects, fish, and worms

Mating: April or May

Nest: No nest; they will use natural cavities in the ground or abandoned burrows of small mammals.

Eggs: No eggs are laid. Eastern garter snakes are born live in a litter of 8–20 snakes.

Young: Snakelets are 4½–9 inches long at birth; no parental care is given.

Predators: Crows, ravens, hawks, owls, raccoons, foxes, and squirrels

Eastern garter snakes are black with three yellow stripes running down their body on the back and sides. They withstand winter by gathering in groups inside the burrows of rodents or under human-made structures, and they enter brumation, or a state of slowed body activity.

Did you know?

The eastern newt starts its life in the water and then lives on land as a juvenile before returning to live out the rest of its life in the water as an adult. Some newts will skip the juvenile stage and change straight into an adult. Eastern newts have a toxin that they release through their skin that makes potential predators sick. The bright-orange color of an eastern newt acts as a warning system to would-be predators that they taste bad or are toxic.

Most Active   Hibernates

Eastern Newt

Notophthalmus viridescens

Size: 3–5 inches long; weighs less than a dime

Habitat: Near and in streams, marshes, lakes, and ponds; in woodlands or woody areas

Range: Throughout much of New York; found from New England and the Atlantic Coast and west as far as Texas

Food: Aquatic insects, snails, worms, amphibians, and fish eggs

Mating: Breeding season for the eastern newt starts in the winter and finishes in early spring.

Nest: No true nest; eggs are laid underwater.

Eggs: Females lay eggs in the spring, in still or quiet water. Eggs attach to underwater vegetation. Females lay 200–400 eggs, providing no form of care.

Young: The larvae hatch around 3–8 weeks after eggs are laid. Larvae transform into efts (juveniles) by the end of summer. Efts live on land for 1–3 years. When mature, they return to the water for the remainder of their lives.

Predators: Fish, birds, insects, amphibians, and reptiles

The eastern newt goes through three life stages. It has a fully aquatic or water-living stage as a larva. During this stage, it has gills and a flat tail. In the next stage (the juvenile stage), it lives on land. This stage of life is called the red eft stage. During this stage, it sports rough, bright-red skin with red spots and has a rounded tail. The last stage is the adult stage, where it has a brownish-yellow-to-olive-brown color on the upper half of the body, red spots outlined by black circles, and a yellow underside with black spots on it.

Did you know?

Five-lined skinks get their name from the five stripes or lines that run down their body. It's a myth that young five-lines are poisonous; while they are not poisonous, their blue color could be used to trick predators into believing that they taste bad. Another use for the blue tail is to act as a distraction. When the five-lined skink is caught, it can drop its tail, and the flopping, brightly colored tail can help aid in its escape.

Most Active   Hibernates

Five-lined Skink

Plestiodon fasciatus

Size: 5–8½ inches long; weighs 4½ ounces

Habitat: Forests, rocky areas, woodlands, and wetlands

Range: They are found in eastern New York and throughout the eastern United States to Florida, west to Texas, and as far north as Canada.

Food: Carnivores (eaters of meat); spiders, newborn mice, frogs, beetles and other insects, and lizards

Nest: Cavity nests are usually made in rotten logs, stumps, rocks, and bark.

Eggs: Lays 15–18 eggs

Young: 4–6 weeks after incubation, the 2–2½-inch-long young hatch. Young are independent at hatching but will receive care and protection for 1–2 days until they leave the nest. Skinks become mature 2–3 years after hatching.

Predators: Birds such as crows, American kestrels, shrikes, and hawks; cats, foxes, raccoons, shrews, snakes, and moles

When young, five-lined skinks are dark brown to black with five yellow-to-off-white lines on their back that run to the base of the tail. Their tail is a brilliant blue. The color of the tail fades as they age, and the lines change from yellow to brown (and some are almost completely gone). The dark-brown color fades, too, and older individuals are often brownish with faint lines. During breeding season, males will don a reddish-orange chin.

Did you know?

The gray tree frog looks similar to the Cope's gray tree frog, and you can only tell them apart by listening to their call or looking at their DNA in a lab. Tree frogs are excellent climbers; they have toe pads that help them to climb trees and other structures.

Most Active   Hibernates

Gray Tree Frog

Dryophytes versicolor

Size: 1½–2¼ inches long; weighs ¼ ounce

Habitat: Urban areas, woodlands, and forests

Range: They can be found throughout New York. They are also found throughout the eastern United States from the Atlantic Coast to middle Texas, and as far north as southern Canada.

Food: Tadpoles: algae and decaying material in bodies of water; adults: insects, spiders, snails, and slugs

Mating: May to July, in shallow wetlands near forest. Males will call to attract females. Males are territorial and will defend territories with force by headbutting, pushing, and/or kicking other males until they leave.

Nest: No nest is constructed; they will lay several clusters containing around 30 eggs or more on vegetation near the surface of a body of water.

Eggs: Lays 1,000–2,000 eggs

Young: Eggs hatch around 3 weeks after being laid; it takes around 4 to 8 weeks after hatching to go through metamorphosis. Young reach maturity at around 2 years.

Predators: Skunks, snakes, raccoons, fish, and other frogs

Gray tree frogs can be a variation of colors from gray to shades of green and brown. They are nocturnal, so they are active at night. In winter, they will hibernate in trees. They will produce glycerol, which is a compound that replaces the water in cells to act as an antifreeze during the winter.

Did you know?
The cricket frog gets its name from the sound that it makes. Its "gick, gick, gick . . . " call sounds like the chirp of a cricket. While small, it has one of the largest jumps; it can jump as long as 5–6 feet. While technically in the tree frog family, you will not catch this frog in trees because it likes to stay on the ground.

Most Active   Hibernates

Northern Cricket Frog

Acris crepitans

Size: 5–1¼ inches long; weighs ¼ ounce

Habitat: Edges of ponds and streams, marshes, cities, lakes, wetlands, woodlands, and forests

Range: They can be found in southeastern New York westward to Texas, as far north to South Dakota and as far south as the panhandle of Florida.

Food: Mosquitoes, spiders, and worms

Mating: May–July

Nest: No nest; eggs are attached to vegetation.

Eggs: Eggs are either laid one at a time or in a cluster of 5–10 at the water surface, attached to vegetation.

Young: Tadpoles hatch within 4 days and take months to turn into frogs. Reproductive maturity is reached in the first year.

Predators: Birds, fish, snakes, and other frogs

The northern cricket frog is North America's smallest frog. It has bumpy skin that comes in a variety of colors, including green, brown, and gray, all with various splotches. Legs have dark bands on them. They have a dark triangle between the eyes and a bright stripe in the shape of a "Y" on their back.

Did you know?

Leopard frogs are used by humans in many ways, including in research for medical projects, as well as serving as specimens for biology courses. During the winter, they will hibernate underwater in ponds that have lots of oxygen and do not freeze.

Most Active   Hibernates

Northern Leopard Frog

Lithobates pipiens

Size: 2½–4½ inches long; weighs ½–3 ounces

Habitat: Meadows, open fields, lakes, forest edges, and ponds

Range: They are found throughout New York; there are strong populations into Canada and throughout the northeastern states to Iowa, with populations extending into northern California, the Pacific Northwest, and the Southwest.

Food: Spiders, worms, insects, and other invertebrates like crustaceans and mollusks

Mating: Late March to early June; mating occurs in water.

Nest: No nest is constructed; within 3 days of mating, the female will lay eggs in permanent shallow bodies of water, attached to vegetation just below the surface.

Eggs: A few hundred to 5,000 or more eggs are laid in one egg mass that is 2–5 inches wide.

Young: Tadpoles hatch about 2–3 weeks after eggs are laid and then complete the metamorphic cycle to become frogs in around 3 months. They reach reproductive maturity in the first or second year for males and within 2–3 years for females.

Predators: Fish, frogs, herons, snakes, hawks, gulls, mink, turtles, and dragonfly larvae

The northern leopard frog is a smooth-skinned frog with 2–3 rows of dark spots with a lighter outline around them, atop a brown or green base layer. It has a ridge that extends from the base of the eye to the rear of the frog. They have a white underside. Juveniles (young) will use streams and drainage ditches with vegetation to reach seasonal habitats.

Did you know?

The queen snake's head is armored. It has nine large scales on the top of its head, and its chin has thick scales that allow it to chase prey under rocks.

Most Active   Hibernates

Queen Snake

Regina septemvittata

Size: 24 inches long; weighs ¼ ounce

Habitat: Urban areas, woodlands, and forests

Range: In New York, they can be found in the eastern part of the state and occasionally in the western area. They can also be found throughout the eastern United States.

Food: Mostly crayfish; frogs, minnows, newts, tadpoles, and snails

Mating: Spring

Nest: No nest is constructed.

Eggs: No eggs; gives live birth to live young

Young: Queen snakes give live birth after 90–120 days to 5–20 snakelets that are about 6 inches long. Baby snakes are independent at birth and will reach reproductive maturity at around 3 years for females and 2 years for males.

Predators: Fish, raccoons, frogs, otters, hawks, mink, other snakes, and herons

Queen snakes are grayish brown to dark brown on their back with yellow-to-pale-peach lines that run down its sides starting at the chin. Queen snakes have four dark stripes that run down their stomach. Juveniles have more stripes than adults, with stripes fading away as they age. Females are a little larger than males.

Did you know?

The snapping turtle's sex is determined by the temperature of the nest! Nest temperatures that are 67–68 degrees produce females, temperatures in the range between 70 and 72 degrees produce both males and females, and nests that are 73–75 degrees will usually produce all males.

Most Active

134

Snapping Turtle, Common

Chelydra serpentina

Size: 8–16 inches long; weighs 10–35 pounds

Habitat: Rivers, marshes, and lakes; can be found in areas that have brackish water (freshwater and saltwater mixture)

Range: They are found throughout New York; also found in the eastern US and southern Canada.

Food: These omnivores (eaters of both plants and animals) eat frogs, reptiles, snakes, birds, small mammals, and plants.

Mating: April to November are the breeding months; lays eggs during June and July.

Nest: Females dig a hole in sandy soil and lay the eggs into it.

Eggs: 25–42 eggs, sometimes as many as 80 or more

Young: Like sea turtles, snapping turtles have temperature-dependent sex determination (TSD), meaning the temperature of the nest determines the sex of the young. Hatchlings leave the nest between August and October. In the North, turtles mature at around 15–20 years, while southern turtles mature around 12 years old.

Predators: Raccoons, skunks, crows, dogs, and humans

The snapping turtle's carapace (top shell) is dark green to brown and usually covered in algae or moss. The plastron (or bottom of the shell) is smaller than the carapace. They are crepuscular animals that are mostly active during the dawn and dusk hours. Young turtles will actively look for food. As adults, they rely heavily on ambushing to hunt; they bury themselves in the sand with just the tip of their nose and eyes showing.

Did you know?

Wood frogs are one of the few amphibians found in the Arctic Circle. They can stop their hearts and breathing when hibernating. They have a special antifreeze that keeps their cells from freezing. Eggs are not harmed by freezing; the eggs that are fertilized will stop developing until the weather warms up.

Most Active

Hibernates

Wood Frog

Lithobates sylvaticus

Size: 2–3¼ inches long; weighs ¼ ounce

Habitat: Bogs, meadows, temporary wetlands, forests, marshes, and swamps

Range: Can be found throughout the United States as far north as Alaska and as far south as Alabama, with range extending westward into Idaho. They can be found throughout New York.

Food: As adults: insects, snails, worms, slugs, and spiders and other arachnids. As tadpoles: vegetation, algae, and decaying plant material

Mating: Early spring in March, sometimes even before ice and snow has started to melt

Nest: No nest; lays eggs in ponds

Eggs: A mass of 1,000–3,000 eggs

Young: Tadpoles hatch 9–30 days after laying. Will turn into frogs in 6–9 weeks and reach reproductive maturity around 1–2 years.

Predators: Snapping turtles, salamanders, raccoons, skunks, beetles, coyotes, foxes, other wood frogs, and birds

Both males and females are brown, dirty red, or tannish in color. They have bumpy skin and a black mask like raccoons or superheroes! They have a pale stomach that is usually yellow to off-white. They have a skin fold that runs down the back from the eyes.

Glossary

Adaptation—An animal's physical (outward) or behavioral (inward) adjustment to changes in the environment.

Amphibian—A small animal with a backbone, has moist skin, and lacks scales. Most amphibians start out as an egg, live at least part of their life in water, and finish life as a land dweller.

Biome—A part or region of Earth that has a particular type of climate and animals and plants that adapted to live in the area.

Bird—A group of animals that all have two legs and feet, a beak, feathers, and wings; while not all birds fly, all birds lay eggs.

Brood—A group of young birds that hatch at the same time and with the same mother.

Carnivore—An animal that primarily eats other animals.

Clutch—The number of eggs an animal lays during one nesting period; an animal can lay more than one clutch each season.

Crepuscular—The hours before sunset or just after sunrise; some animals have adapted to be most active during these low-light times.

Diurnal—During the day; many animals are most active during the daytime.

Ecosystem—A group of animals and plants that interact with each other and the physical area that they live in.

Evolution—A process of change in a species or a group of animals that are all the same kind; evolution happens over several generations or in a group of animals living around the same time; evolution happens through adaptation, or physical and biological changes to better fit the environment over time.

Fledgling—A baby bird that has developed flight feathers and has left the nest.

Gestation—The length of time a developing animal is carried in its mother's womb.

Herbivore—An animal that primarily eats plants.

Hibernate—A survival strategy or process where animals "slow down" and go into a long period of reduced activity to survive winter or seasonal changes; during hibernation, activities like feeding, breathing, and converting food to energy all stop.

Insectivore—An animal whose diet consists of insects.

Incubate—When a bird warms eggs by sitting on them.

Invasive—A nonnative animal that outcompetes native animals in a particular area, harming the environment.

Mammal—An air-breathing, warm-blooded, fur- or hair-covered animal with a backbone. All mammals produce milk and usually give birth to live young.

Migration—When animals move from one area to another. Migration usually occurs seasonally, but it can also happen due to biological processes, such as breeding.

Molt—When animals shed or drop their skin, feathers, or shell.

Nocturnal—At night; many animals are most active at night.

Piscivore—An animal that eats mainly fish.

Predator—An animal that hunts (and eats) other animals.

Raptor—A group of birds that all have a curved beak and sharp talons; they hunt or feed on other animals. Also known as a bird of prey.

Reptile—An egg-laying, air-breathing, cold-blooded animal that has a backbone and skin made of scales, which crawls on its belly or uses stubby legs to get around.

Scat—The waste product that animals release from their bodies; another word for it is poop or droppings.

Talon—The claw on the feet seen on raptors and birds of prey.

Torpor—A form of hibernation in which an animal slows down its breathing and heart rate; torpor ranges from a few hours at a time to a whole day; torpor does not involve a deep sleep.

Checklist

Mammals

- ☐ American Beaver
- ☐ American Marten
- ☐ Black Bear
- ☐ Bobcat
- ☐ Coyote
- ☐ Eastern Chipmunk
- ☐ Eastern Cottontail
- ☐ Eastern Fox Squirrel
- ☐ Harbor Seal
- ☐ Humpback Whale
- ☐ Indiana Bat
- ☐ Long-tailed Weasel
- ☐ Mink
- ☐ Moose
- ☐ Northern Long-eared Bat
- ☐ Northern Raccoon
- ☐ Northern River Otter
- ☐ Red Fox
- ☐ Striped Skunk
- ☐ Virginia Opossum
- ☐ White-tailed Deer

Birds

- ☐ American Goldfinch
- ☐ American Kestrel
- ☐ American Robin
- ☐ American Woodcock
- ☐ Bald Eagle
- ☐ Barred Owl
- ☐ Belted Kingfisher
- ☐ Black-capped Chickadee
- ☐ Bobolink
- ☐ Canada Goose
- ☐ Common Loon
- ☐ Double-crested Cormorant
- ☐ Eastern Bluebird
- ☐ Eastern Meadowlark
- ☐ Great Blue Heron
- ☐ Great Horned Owl
- ☐ Hairy/Downy Woodpecker
- ☐ Hooded Merganser
- ☐ Mallard
- ☐ Mourning Dove
- ☐ Northern Cardinal

- [ ] Osprey
- [ ] Peregrine Falcon
- [ ] Red-tailed Hawk/
  Red-shouldered Hawk
- [ ] Red-winged Blackbird
- [ ] Short-eared Owl
- [ ] Snowy Owl
- [ ] Trumpeter Swan
- [ ] Wild Turkey
- [ ] Wood Duck

Reptiles and Amphibians

- [ ] American Toad
- [ ] Bog Turtle
- [ ] Eastern Box Turtle
- [ ] Eastern Garter Snake
- [ ] Eastern Newt
- [ ] Five-lined Skink
- [ ] Gray Tree Frog
- [ ] Northern Cricket Frog
- [ ] Northern Leopard Frog
- [ ] Queen Snake
- [ ] Snapping Turtle, Common
- [ ] Wood Frog

The Art of Conservation®

Featuring two signature programs, The Songbird Art Contest™ and The Fish Art Contest®, the Art of Conservation programs celebrate the arts as a cornerstone to conservation. To enter, youth artists create an original hand-drawn illustration and written essay, story, or poem synthesizing what they have learned. The contests are FREE to enter and open to students in K-12. For program updates, rules, guidelines, and entry forms, visit: www.TheArtofConservation.org.

The Fish Art Contest® introduces youth to the wonders of fish, the joy of fishing, and the importance of aquatic conservation. The Fish Art Contest uses art, science, and creative writing to foster connections to the outdoors and inspire the next generation of stewards. Participants are encouraged to use the Fish On! lesson plan, then submit an original, handmade piece of artwork to compete for prizes and international recognition.

The Songbird Art Contest® explores the wonders and species diversity of North American songbirds. Raising awareness and educating the public on bird conservation, the Songbird program builds stewardship, encourages outdoors participation, and promotes the discovery of nature.

Photo Credits

Stewart Ragan: 144
Silhouettes and tracks by Anthony Hertzel unless otherwise noted.
s=silhouette ; t=animal track(s)

These images are used under the CC0 1.0 Universal (CC 1.0) Public Domain Dedication license, which can be found at www.creativecommons.org/publicdomain/zero/1.0/: **NABat_John Lamb:** 41; **NABat/Will Seiter/Copperhead Environmental Consulting Inc.:** 33; **NABat/Diane Smith:** 32; **USFWS/Jill Utrup:** 40

This image is used under Attribution 2.0 Generic (CC BY 2.0) license, which can be found at https://creativecommons.org/licenses/by/2.0/: **Judy Gallagher:** 136, original image at https://www.flickr.com/photos/52450054@N04/52292746501/

All images used under license from Shutterstock.com:

John L. Absher: 96; **ace03:** footer burst; **Robert Adami:** 90; **Tristan Adler:** 38; **Airin.dizain:** 42s; **Muhammad Alfatih 05:** 18s; **Md. Ershad Ali:** 26; **Alpha C:** 26s, 48s; **Lukasz Antoniszyn:** 37; **Victor Arita:** 19; **Agnieszka Bacal:** 70; **Raul Baena:** 55; **Barry Barnes:** 8 (state motto); **Bonnie Taylor Barry:** 94; **basel101658:** 36s; **Michael Benard:** 123; **Gabbie Berry:** 122; **Roman Bjuty:** 29; **Karel Bock:** 131; **Todd Boland:** 111; **Miles Boyer:** 114; **Larry Burk:** 127; **Mark Byer:** 39; **Steve Byland:** 69, 79; **Patrick K. Campbell:** 124; **Mark Castiglia:** 17; **Phoo Chan:** 77; **yongsheng chen:** 84; **Romuald Cisakowski:** 34; **Mircea Costina:** 52, 71, 121; **DarAnna:** 91; **Gerald A. DeBoer:** 51; **Steven D_Cruze:** 104; **Danita Delimont:** 56; **DnDavis:** 85; **Dominate Studio:** 12s; **Dennis W Donohue:** 24, 80; **dramaj:** 40s; **Ian Duffield:** 100; **Kozyreva Elena:** 34s; **Eroshka:** 50s; **Nico Faramaz:** 31; **Deborah Ferrin:** 21; **Frank Fichtmueller:** 13; **FloridaStock:** 62; **Jiri Foltyn:** 23; **FotoRequest:** 14, 54, 64, 87; **Lev Frid:** 133; **Vlad G:** 8 (American beaver); **Gallinago_media:** 46s; **Ghost Bear:** 35; **Colin Gillette:** 126; **Bildagentur Zoonar GmbH:** 49; **Greens and Blues:** 106; **Elliotte Rusty Harold:** 44; **Harry Collins Photography:** 46, 67, 98, 105, 112; **Ayman Haykal:** 59; **Ray Hennessy:** 75; **Karen Hogan:** 86; **Malachi Ives:** 65; **Joseph Scott Photography:** 83; **Paul Jones Jr:** 72; **Tory Kallman:** 110; **KBel:** 30s; **David Byron Keener:** 125; **Keneva Photography:** 88; **Breck P. Kent:** 128, 129; **Janet M Kessler:** 58; **Krumpelman Photography:** 89, 102; **Geoffrey Kuchera:** 48; **Holly Kuchera:** 59; **Francisco Martinez Lanzas:** 36; **Brian Lasenby:** 66, 74, 134; **Felix Lipov:** 8 (state nickname); **L-N:** 43; **mamita:** 20s; **Don Mammoser:** 18, 101, 108; **Karl R. Martin:** 82; **Kazakova Maryia:** 11 (ground nest); **Matthew R McClure:** 8 (bay scallop); **Martin Mecnarowski:** 97; **Alyssa Metro:** 130; **Elly Miller:** 63; **Miloje:** background/inset burst; **Matthieu Moingt:** 92; **MurzillA:** 38s; **Christian Musat:** 12; **Nagel Photography:** 109; **natmac stock:** 137; **nialat:** 45; **Jay Ondreicka:** 116, 117; **Paul Reeves Photography:** 42, 115; **Nick Pecker:** 50; **pichayasri:** 11 (platform nest), 11 (suitcase); **Dimitrios Pippis:** 119; **Travis Potter:** 15; **Rabbitti:** 25, 78; **Dalton Rasmussen:** 61; **Leena Robinson:** 27, 57; **Romeo Guzman Photography:** 81; **Jason Patrick Ross:** 120, 132; **RT Images:** 107; **Kyle Selcer:** 8 (sugar maple); **Menno Schaefer:** 47; **George Schmiesing:** 22, 103; **Alan B. Schroeder:** 8 (eastern bluebird); **SCStock:** 16; **Shoriful_is:** 95; **Anzhela Shvab:** 8 (wild rose); **Benjamin Simeneta:** 135; **slowmotiongli:** 8 (brook trout); **Andrea J Smith:** 60; **SofiaV:** 11 (cavity nest); **Harold Stiver:** 93; **stopkin:** 16s; **Marek R. Swadzba:** 73; **Taxomony:** 8 (ladybug); **T_Dub0v:** 11 (cup nest); **Paul Tessier:** 53; **Earth theater:** 30; **Thomas Torget:** 20; **Suzanne Tucker:** 118; **Vector412:** 28s; **vectoric:** basketball; **Viktorya170377:** 22s; **w e s o m e 24:** 24s; **Wirestock Creators:** 76; **Brian Woolman:** 8 (common snapping turtle); **ya_mayka:** 44s; **yhelfman:** 28; **yvontrep:** 68; **Oral Zirek:** 113

About the Author

Alex Troutman is a wildlife biologist, birder, nature enthusiast, and science communicator from Austell, Georgia. He has a passion for sharing the wonders of nature and introducing the younger generation to the outdoors. He holds both a bachelor's degree and a master's degree in biology from Georgia Southern University (the Real GSU), with a focus in conservation.  Because he knows what it feels like to not see individuals who look like you (or come from a similar background) doing the things you enjoy or working in the career that you aspire to be in, Alex makes a point not only to be that representation for the younger generation, but also to make sure that kids have exposure to the careers they are interested in and the diverse scientists working in those careers.

Alex is the co-organizer of several Black in X weeks, including Black Birders Week, Black Mammologists Week, and Black in Marine Science Week. This movement encourages diversity in nature, the celebration of Black individual scientists, awareness of Black nature enthusiasts, and diversity in STEAM fields.

ABOUT ADVENTUREKEEN

We are an independent nature and outdoor activity publisher. Our founding dates back more than 40 years, guided then and now by our love of being in the woods and on the water, by our passion for reading and books, and by the sense of wonder and discovery made possible by spending time recreating outdoors in beautiful places. It is our mission to share that wonder and fun with our readers, especially with those who haven't yet experienced all the physical and mental health benefits that nature and outdoor activity can bring. #bewellbeoutdoors